# A Rare Titanic Family

ALSO BY JULIE HEDGEPETH WILLIAMS

*Wings of Opportunity: The Wright Brothers in
Montgomery, Alabama, 1910* (2010)

*The Significance of the Printed Word in Early America:
Colonists' Thoughts on the Role of the Press* (1999)

*The Early American Press, 1690–1783*
(1994, co-author with William David Sloan)

*The Great Reporters: An Anthology of News Writing at Its Best*
(1992, co-author with William David Sloan,
Patricia C. Place, and Kevin Stoker)

# A RARE TITANIC FAMILY

## The Caldwells' Story of Survival

JULIE HEDGEPETH WILLIAMS

NEWSOUTH BOOKS

Montgomery

NewSouth Books
105 S. Court Street
Montgomery, AL 36104

Library of Congress Cataloging-in-Publication Data

Williams, Julie Hedgepeth.
A rare Titanic family : the Caldwells' story of survival / Julie Hedgepeth Williams.
p. cm.
Includes bibliographical references and index.
ISBN 978-1-58838-282-5 — ISBN 1-58838-282-6
1. Titanic (Steamship) 2. Shipwrecks—North Atlantic Ocean. 3. Caldwell family.
4. Shipwreck survival. I. Title.
G530.T6W54 2012
910.9163'4—dc23

2011044854

Design by Randall Williams
Printed in the United States of America

*Read about Sylvia Caldwell's experiences on the Titanic in her own words.*
Women of the Titanic Disaster *by Sylvia Caldwell—available in*
*ebook format at www.newsouthbooks.com/caldwell*

IN MEMORY OF
ALBERT, SYLVIA, AND ALDEN

DEDICATED TO THOSE WHO KNEW THE CALDWELLS, ESPECIALLY:
KAY AND LLOYD HEDGEPETH
JAN WRIGHT AND ANNE HEDGEPETH
THE CONGLETONS AND ROMEISERS
CHARLES "CHUCK" CALDWELL
AND CAROLYN ELWESS, WHO SHOULD HAVE KNOWN THEM

AND FOR MY OWN SON ALDEN,
WHO SO PROUDLY BEARS THE NAME

# Contents

# A Vast Ocean of Things
# I Didn't Know

I set out to tell a story that I thought I knew as well as my own name—the story of my great-uncle Albert Caldwell and how he survived the *Titanic*. I knew "Uncle Al," as I called him, very well and heard the *Titanic* story from him multiple times. He lived to be ninety-one and died in 1977 when I was a senior in high school; I was old enough to develop a deep and permanent interest in this rarest of firsthand accounts.

However, the story turned out to be far rarer than Uncle Al had ever hinted. Al's *Titanic* memorabilia came to my mother after he died, and his collection implied that there were parts of the story that my family and I had never known. There was, for instance, Al's picture of himself; his wife, Sylvia; and their baby, Alden, on the deck of the *Titanic*. None of us had ever seen it. Eventually I tracked down Alden, whom I did not know, as Al had long ago divorced Sylvia and later had married my great-aunt Jennie Congleton. We were, therefore, Al's second family, and we had no real connection to the first. Despite that gap, Alden was gracious in answering my questions and was pleased to see the picture again. I also tracked down his younger brother, Raymond, who likewise was thoughtful and delighted about the picture. But there were questions I didn't ask before it was too late for them, either, and I regretted that none of the Caldwells lived long enough to know that I named my own son Alden in honor of my *Titanic* family.

My own Alden was fourteen before the secrets that his namesake family had held so tightly began to crack open under the scrutiny of research. I was astonished to find out that the Caldwells' trip on the *Titanic* was one leg of an around-the-world escape from Siam to New York, with the Caldwells being hounded by, of all parties, the Presbyterian church. The Caldwells said they were running from Siam (now called Thailand) to save Sylvia's health and sanity, while key churchmen suspected the Caldwells were fleeing under contrived circumstances and thus were contractually bound to repay the church a forbiddingly enormous sum of money. It took the *Titanic* to resolve the struggle.

BUT NONE OF THE surprising facts or the rich story behind them was obvious at the outset. As I tried to fill in what I thought were a few small gaps in my knowledge of the Caldwells' *Titanic* story, I turned to cyber-space and happily stumbled upon two key people. First was Carolyn McHenry Elwess, the archivist for Park University, where Albert and Sylvia met in 1904 when it was still called Park College. Park was pivotal in Sylvia and Albert's *Titanic* story. Not only did they meet there, but the college also helped set up the Caldwells as idealistic missionaries to Siam, an assignment from which they eventually fled via the ill-fated ship. Carolyn had done excellent research into the Caldwells' student days. Her ongoing cascade of information from college publications and Park University's Fishburn Archives was a godsend. Carolyn also put me in touch with Charles "Chuck" Caldwell, the Caldwells' grandson, who jumped in with family memories. Particularly valuable was his knowledge of Sylvia, whom I knew little about. Chuck's childhood memories and stash of family pictures were essential, as was his insightfully scientific approach that featured thoughtful logic and careful analysis. His many contacts in the world of *Titanic* researchers and his genealogical searches were invaluable. I rounded out the *Titanic* Trio, or *Titanic* Troika, as Carolyn called us, as I had known Albert well enough to consider him a grandfather. He had been brother-in-law to my own grandfather, Will Congleton, who died before I was born. Albert treated me like a granddaughter, stepping in where Will Congleton could not.

As much as Chuck, Carolyn, and I knew about the Caldwells, we quickly came to realize how much we had *not* known. As Chuck summed it up, "The more I find out, the less I know." He certainly spoke for me in that case. It has been a marvelous trek through Al's personal papers, Sylvia's writings, the Presbyterian Historical Society, relatives' memories, contacts with archivists and historians, the internet, and lots of theories, rejection of theories, dilemmas, discouragements, and delights, along with fine discussion by *Titanic* Trio. This book would not have been written without the help of the other two members of the Trio, but any misinterpretations or errors in stating information are my own, not Chuck's or Carolyn's or any other contributor's.

I must thank David Sloan for suggesting I do the book. So many other people played key roles, too: Bill Romeiser's audiotape of Al was priceless; Jim Congleton passed along information on a supposed bribe by Al aboard the *Titanic*; Liz Wells helped me date a pair of baby shoes that may have been Alden's on the *Titanic*. Others furnished first-person accounts, photos, articles, and key information from the Caldwells' era: Dan Barringer, George Behe, Robert Cisneros, Vera Williams Congleton, Dick Johnson, Jacky Johnson, Ed Kamuda, Bill Kemp, Dave Knopf, Bruce Parrish, Heather Richmond, John Robertson, and Virginia Congleton Romeiser. Several key people—Anne Conybeare Trach, Marcia A. Trach, Suda Carey, Mike Flannery, and Darryl Lee Salter—helped me grasp the Siam experience. I relied on technical assistance from Paula Noles (the genealogy wizard) and Gail Barton (the microfilm wizard). The map of the Caldwells' route by my sister Jan Hedgepeth Wright and her daughter Eleanor Wright truly brought the Caldwells' world to life. The rigorous analysis and thoughtful questions by my husband, Evan J. Williams, meant so much. My son Weston Williams was awfully tolerant to let me work out issues in the manuscript by talking them out loud as we drove to school each day. And a committee of old college friends, including Sarah Taylor and Wendy Gilmer, was so diligent in helping come up with the subtitle.

I want to add my deep appreciation for the multitude of other *Titanic* scholars who have studied many aspects of the ship's short but infamous career. They have done intricate research and dazzling analysis. I may have relied on some of them here, but in the main I have not mentioned various points about the *Titanic* if the Caldwells didn't seem to be aware of them. I relied mostly on the Caldwells' vision, whether accurate or flawed.

As I worked on the research into that vast ocean of things I did not know, I spent a delightful spring break with my childhood family by the Atlantic in North Carolina, not too far from where Al Caldwell is buried. As we shivered through a chilly week, we recalled Uncle Al. My mother, Kay Congleton Hedgepeth, was Al's niece by marriage and one of his heirs. My father, Lloyd Hedgepeth, had been so close to Al that Al took him aside the night before my parents' wedding, saying, "I'm the oldest one here, so we need to have a little talk." He proceeded to give my father the birds and bees talk, which we all found hilarious and so Al-like, especially since Dad had already had "the talk" from his own father. "Well," Dad quipped, "Al *was* the oldest one there!" Al considered Dad like a son, just as he had long considered my mother to be like a daughter. When Mom was a child, Al was often part of her life, whether treating her to the automat food vendor (an amazement for a small-town girl) or listening to her piano practice (the ultimate sacrifice for a parent-figure) or making up silly lyrics to her recital piece, the morbidly titled "Dolly's Funeral."

During that cold beach week, my sisters, Jan Wright and Anne Hedgepeth, contributed their memories of Al and his *Titanic* stories and then joined me in a fruitless search through the internet to determine if perhaps Sylvia had been pregnant on the *Titanic*, our momentary notion as to why various crewmen encouraged Al to pass to or get on board the lifeboat on that fateful April night in 1912. By the time it got to 2:20 A.M., we remembered the *Titanic* had sunk at 2:20 as well, and it was time for bed. Our pregnancy theory, like so many others, sank as quickly as the *Titanic* did, but we had a lot of fun tossing about theories and memories.

As we finally concluded during that spring break week, memory is a very slippery fish. Whether it was our memory or Al's as he left to us personally or Sylvia's through her published accounts or through their grandson, or whether it was through the archives at Park University or at the Presbyterian Historical Society, it was clear that no two memories were exactly the same. In fact, sometimes the same story told by the same person in two different interviews varied a little or a lot. As I wrote, I had to figure out which version of the story was the most accurate. I generally tried first to take words straight from Albert and Sylvia and people they knew or met, and the closer to the time period the better. After that I relied on interviews with people in various branches of Albert's and Sylvia's families—people who had heard the story of the *Titanic* from them—followed last by information from later historians. I hope I have chosen well and have made critical discrepancies clear. Sometimes I had to guess based on the wispiest evidence, and I have tried to explain those educated guesses in the text or the source notes. Except where changes were necessary for clarity, I retained original spelling and punctuation in quoted material.

At first, the information about the Caldwells seemed to be a mishmash of facts, questions, and confusion. When the tangled threads were straightened out as much as they could be, however, they made a rich and colorful tapestry of the Caldwells' lives.

The story recounted here, as many people collectively remember it, is the best that fallible memories can produce.

THE ORIGINAL MANUSCRIPT OF *A Rare Titanic Family* includes 780 footnotes. As my publisher pointed out, most readers don't want to read so many notes. On the other hand, the publisher understood that *Titanic* historians might want to know intricate details of sources, especially where the Caldwells' accounts—as they came to me—seem to deviate from other accounts of the *Titanic*.

Thus the footnotes have been preserved in an alternate edition, befitting of the internet age: the fully footnoted manuscript lives on as an ebook and is available at www.newsouthbooks.com/titanic.

Meanwhile, we agreed I would write a narrative essay about my sources to tell general readers where my information came from. That essay appears at the end of this edition. I regret already that I had to leave out some sources in that shortened account. I am grateful to each of my sources, whether they are included in the source essay or only appear in the full footnoted version.

# A Rare Titanic Family

# I

# Of Those in Peril on the Sea

Albert Francis Caldwell, twenty-six, shifted his baby son to one side and peered over the steep side of the ship into . . . nothing. He could see the vertical hull as it slithered into empty darkness, but he couldn't even make out the water below. It was utterly black, void—and, well, puzzling. With baby Alden squirming against the cold night air, Albert wondered why they would be putting women and children off in the lifeboats?

Albert tested the ship beneath his feet, one of those things you do unconsciously every time you step on deck, but this time he thought of it. It was, as his unconscious feet always read it, solid. It wasn't listing. Clearly the ship could not be in any danger. If it were sinking, he'd have tripped over a sloping floor. He'd have heard the rush of water or the screams of panic—all those things you imagine would be evident on a sinking ship. Not one was happening. Clearly, he thought a little crossly, this was a case of overcautious behavior that could result in raw tragedy. Put women and children off in an open boat into an ocean blacker than coal? What a stupid idea!

Albert's thoughts flew to his wife, Sylvia Mae Harbaugh Caldwell, twenty-eight, and to the little son in his arms, Alden, who had turned ten months old just four days before—no, five days, as surely it was now after midnight. Sylvia was getting over a dire illness and was prone to nausea. If she got into an open boat in the Atlantic, she'd become seasick. And the baby? Their precious Alden was small enough to need constant attention, and at this sleepy hour of the night, they hadn't been able to find the key to their trunk —and Alden's warm things were locked in the trunk. Thus the baby was wrapped in a steamer rug. It was warm enough, but it was not his own little coat. Sylvia couldn't even hold the baby properly, owing to the illness she was still battling. The thought of putting the baby on a lifeboat

3

in this bitter cold without his coat when his seasick mother couldn't really hang onto him—well, it was preposterous.

It was obvious to Albert what they needed to do. He had made his decision. He would *not* put his wife and child off on the lifeboat. They would stay on the *Titanic*.

In the two and a half short years of his married life and career, Albert Francis Caldwell had worn various hats—husband, missionary, teacher, father. On this unforgivingly bitter April night in the North Atlantic Ocean, he was looking at the situation entirely as a good husband and father, protecting his wife and child. What he didn't realize, as he shivered to a decision in the darkness, was that the hat he needed to be wearing that night was his missionary one. Because at the moment of that fatal decision, what the Caldwell family needed more than a husband or a daddy was a guardian angel—a sweaty, grimy guardian angel covered in coal dust.

IF ANY COUPLE WERE equipped to recognize a guardian angel, it should have been Albert and Sylvia Caldwell. They had prepared for as long as they could remember for this moment—this critical snap of God's fingers when they needed to recognize miraculous intervention the instant it happened.

Albert was the son of a Presbyterian minister. In fact, the Reverend William Elliott Caldwell was waiting for them at home in Biggsville, Illinois, where he was shepherding the latest in a long string of small churches he had pastored throughout the Midwest. Albert's mother, Fannie, was also waiting, anxious to meet her grandson for the first time. She was named Frances, or "Fannie," after her parents, Francis P. and Mary Frances Gates. William E. and Fannie had named their son Albert Francis for his grandparents and his mother. Born September 8, 1885, at Sanborn, Iowa, Albert was their first child and would be their only son. He contracted pneumonia when he was a toddler but pulled through that, God be thanked. He hadn't really been sick since, another thing to glorify God for. Little Albert seemed on track to follow in the family business, the ministry. He joined the church when he was a small boy.

For Albert's first birthday, he got, of all things, a baby girl named Stella Dennis, also born September 8. He didn't know her just then; she was born

*Albert Francis Caldwell as a baby in Iowa.*

in Kansas and had not actually met anyone in his family yet. However, by the time she was eight she had come to live with them in Allerton, Iowa, after her mother, Caroline Howard Dennis, had died young, and her father, Henry Clay Dennis, had given her up. Caroline had managed to leave her daughter some property, probably jewelry, that was valuable enough to be taxed. William and Fannie didn't let that fact go to Stella's head. They established important routines at home, such as getting down on the knees every night to pray for God's grace for loved ones. By 1895, Albert and Stella had a new person to pray for, Albert's cute baby sister Vera, who for once did *not* arrive on September 8.

But Albert's and Stella's and Vera's growing-up years weren't entirely taken up in seriousness and Bible-reading. There was fun in the household,

*William and Fannie Caldwell at their home in Iowa. Blurred at the bottom are (probably) Albert and Stella. Stella D. Caldwell's exact relationship to the William E. Caldwell family remains a mystery.*

too, including lots of music. A particular favorite was the old English folk song "O the Mistletoe Bough." Albert loved singing the deceitfully holiday-spirited lyrics:

> The mistletoe hung in the castle hall,
> The holly branch shone on the old oak wall;
> And the baron's retainers were blithe and gay,
> All keeping their Christmas holiday.
> The baron beheld, with a father's pride,
> His beautiful child, young Lovell's bride,
> While she with her bright eyes seemed to be,
> The star of the goodly company.
> *O . . . the Mistletoe bough!*
> *O . . . the Mistletoe bough!*

In the ballad the young bride suggested they play hide and seek, but Lovell, alas, could not find her, nor could anyone else . . . and they never did. Lovell aged to old manhood, broken and weeping for his lost bride. The song went on:

> At length an old chest, that had long lain hid,
> Was found in the castle. They raised the lid,
> And a skeleton form lay mouldering there,
> In the bridal wreath of a lady fair.
> Oh, sad was her fate! in sportive jest
> She hid from her lord in an old oak chest;
> It closed with a spring! and her bridal bloom
> Lay withering there in a living tomb.

Albert leaned into the eerie, unhappy refrain one more time, perhaps making little Vera shiver:

> *O . . . the Mistletoe bough!*
> *O . . . the Mistletoe bough!*

The children may have read *Parlor Amusements for the Young Folks*, and if so, the book gave step-by-step directions for acting out the Mistletoe Bough story. Perhaps Albert and Stella played the tragic roles for William and Fannie and little Vera. The book warned children that the girl playing the bride was to hide in a box that was held together only by hook-and-eye latches. This was ostensibly so that the "bride" could be replaced by "mouldering" flowers at the end, although the real object was to keep from repeating Mrs. Lovell's unhappy demise.

Pastor Caldwell didn't make all that much money, but there was enough to hire a live-in housekeeper, Elsie B. Able, just two years older than Albert. Also in the family was Fannie's father, Francis Gates, who lived with them. The three Caldwell children learned with some pride that a Caldwell ancestor had, generations back in the family tree, married into the family of the famous Pilgrim John Alden. It was a family legend that got told around, but no one really knew for sure if it was true. Still, Albert was proud of it.

Albert and Stella shared something else besides their birthday and their household; William's wandering career resulted in the twin-like pair enrolling in high school at the same time, despite the year's difference in their ages. By then the family had moved to Breckenridge, Missouri, in the coincidentally named Caldwell County. Breckenridge was "a hustling little city" of 1,200 people, conveniently located on the railroad and "surrounded by as fine prairie land as the eye could wish to see," bragged a county directory of the era. As one observer put it, the town of Breckenridge had "made a steady, though not rapid growth.... Breckenridge has, however, in the past few years awakened to the necessity of doing things." Just about the time Albert and Stella left home, the town created a "nice park with grand stand and paved walks and a goodly lot of granitoid walks and crossings." The town even boasted telephones, and the year after Albert and Stella went off to college, city voters approved $10,000 (the equivalent of $243,417 in today's dollars) in bonds to build an electric light plant. Whereas Albert and Stella had studied by flame light, young Vera would have electricity.

REVEREND CALDWELL PASTORED THE Presbyterian church in Breckenridge. The congregation met in a frame building and had "a fair membership," as the county directory described it. The good pastor had a lot of competition in converting and comforting souls. The biggest church in town, the Christian church, featured an impressive brick building. The Methodist Episcopal church was smaller but still had an enviable congregation of a hundred people. There was another Methodist Episcopal church in town, plus Baptist, Congregational, and Catholic churches. The town featured seven men's clubs and one women's club, and if Albert hadn't been intended for the ministry or some other sort of church work, he might have grown up to work for the town's self-made entrepreneur, Mr. Ward, who ran a furniture factory.

The Caldwell children were enrolled in the Breckenridge school, a two-story brick affair that flamboyantly featured four smaller bell towers and one huge one, with arched windows and a mansard roof. There were 240 students divided among six teachers, and in 1904 there were fourteen high school seniors. The school served a small town, but it had a curriculum that seemed worthy of any city. Stella reported her course work as:

> Higher Algebra, Phillips and Fisher's Plane and Solid Geometry, Collar and Daniell's First Latin Book, 4 books of Caesar and 4 Orations of Cicero against Citaline. One year of Higher English and one of Rhetoric. Elements of Physical Geography and Geology, Meyers' General History and English, History by Lancaster. American Lit. (Simon and Hawthorne's) and Painter's English Literature. Part I of Crocket's Trigonometry. One year of Civil Government.

The school was imbued with the forward-looking spirit of the frontier that tended toward gender equality. Girls at Breckenridge High took just as much charge of class business as boys—in fact, even more than the boys. This was the twentieth century, after all. Lenora Reynolds was the class president, with Stella serving as class secretary and Ethel Cox handling the class's money as treasurer. The only male officer was Eugene W. Robinson, the vice president.

Breckenridge School's high school department was run under the watchful eye of Principal G. W. Sears and teacher Carrie Kelley. Vera was enrolled

*The Breckenridge school.*

in the lower grades under the tutelage of Mrs. Helen Kirtley. The best part, however, was that Superintendent Nelson Kerr was an advocate of playgrounds and playtime for schoolchildren as part of the normal school day. Kerr believed that play built character in children. Play, he was convinced, kept down thievery and mean-spirited pranks, a theory he was eventually lauded for in a national education magazine. "Do you know, since we have had play as part of the work in the Pitman School [with Kerr as principal] that there have been no gangs of boys on the streets at night?" a banker in Kirkwood, Missouri, exulted eleven years later. "They used to break windows, jeer at passersby and destroy property in various petty ways."

Accordingly, the school in Breckenridge offered healthy fun as well as work. Albert and Stella studied under that strenuous curriculum but also enjoyed the more pleasant aspects of education. Albert was a singer, good enough and confident enough to perform a vocal solo during one of the graduation events their senior year. Stella read the Class Will as part of the festivities, while classmates Ethel and Minnie Cox performed a "Comedietta" entitled "Graduating Essays." The school had an orchestra, which played in honor of the graduates on Class Day. All fourteen seniors performed the class song and took part in a pantomime.

Albert himself prepared an oration, "Night Brings Forth the Stars." The speech doubtlessly spoke of the outpouring of star power from the class itself. The Class Prophecy, delivered by Wynne Curran, probably did not foretell tragic decisions regarding lifeboats in the mid-Atlantic, although no doubt it did anticipate success and great futures. Curran himself went on to study engineering. Classmate Joseph Howard Peck became a doctor. As the Class of 1904 set forth into the world, the future took on the sparkle of the new century as predicted by the title of Albert's speech.

The Class of 1904 of Breckenridge School chose blue and white as their class colors—the colors of puffy clouds and the vibrant sky hovering above the green hills of Caldwell County—and the violet as the class flower. Albert, however, did not intend to stay amongst those green hills. He had spent his childhood moving about, and he was not sentimentally tied to the place. He intended to get a college education, even though his parents didn't have enough money to pay for a typical college course. Albert already knew how he'd lick that problem. He would work his way through Park College, the Presbyterian school that took in penniless (or practically penniless) students. It was only eighty miles away by railroad, but ultimately it would take him around the world, concluding with a catastrophic trip on the *Titanic*.

Meanwhile, Sylvia Harbaugh was on a similar trajectory. She, too, was the daughter of a devout Presbyterian family, and according to one source, her father, Chambers C. Harbaugh, had been born in China, which indicated he was a missionary's son (even though the U.S. Census persisted in reporting he was born in the very ordinary location of Pennsylvania). He had been a drover when he was a young man but later was an oil company salesman and now was a clerk in Glenshaw, a rural suburb of Pittsburgh. Sylvia was born in Pittsburgh on July 23, 1883 or 1885, the second of five children, four of them girls. Her older sister was Alice; then there was Sylvia, who was named for her mother; followed by younger sister Beatrice. Then came brother Milton, and finally little Eva.

ALICE STARTED SCHOOL AT the old Shaw Mill building in Glenshaw, but Sylvia probably started in the brand new Glenshaw School, built in 1889. It featured four rooms and was forced to add four more before the decade was out. A large, airy cupola atop held the school bell, and chimneys dotted the four corners. It was a fine building but, alas, did not offer high school in time to serve the Harbaughs. If Alice wanted a high school education, she'd have to go elsewhere. The school cobbled together a two-year high school course in 1900, and possibly Sylvia enrolled, but a year later, she had left Glenshaw for good to go to school. By the end of her public school days in her hometown, however, Sylvia had completed coursework in "physiology, geography, mental, . . . and Barnes' History. Will complete Franklin's Complete Arithmetic, Reid & Kellogg's grammar, algebra and speller, and the greater part of Civil Govt," and, she added hopefully, "My teacher has offered to help me with Latin."

Sylvia was, by her own description, "reared in a Christian home. I have always attended Sunday School and church." She joined the Presbyterian church in Glenshaw in 1899 when she was a teenager, and at various points in her youth joined church groups including the Missionary Society and Christian Endeavor, which she served as president. The Presbyterian church in Glenshaw was a major focus of the community. It started out in an abandoned sickle factory in 1853, and despite such humble origins, it took root. Its handsome new building, featuring a latticework bell tower, was put up in 1887 at a cost of $12,000 ($276,168 today). Sylvia was steeped in a missionary tradition even in unexotic Glenshaw. The year she joined Glenshaw Presbyterian, the Reverend William F. Plummer reported that the church had been involved in mission work for the past twenty years, and in 1899, the congregation raised $441.22 ($10,343 today) for mission projects.

Being a Presbyterian in Glenshaw, Sylvia almost couldn't help but be bookish. The town featured the oldest public library west of the Allegheny Mountains, its first volume having been checked out in 1888. In fact, the library started at Glenshaw Presbyterian when congregants circulated books after Sunday School. In 1895, the people of Glenshaw held a book party to increase the numbers of books available. They got enough to move the library to a building everyone called "the White Elephant" around 1900. Some books that the Harbaugh children might have checked out included *The Boys of '76*, published a century after the American Revolution in honor of that great conflict. They might have leafed through the book next to the model of the Mayflower that was displayed in the library to remind people of the even more distant American past. In 1886 they might have checked out Charles Lamb's brand new *Essays of Elia*; and by the 1890s the Harbaughs could check out new acquisitions such as *Moths and Butterflies* by Julia P. Dallard; Dr. Edward Brooks' analysis of Homer's *Iliad*; and *Timothy's Quest* by Kate Douglas Wiggin, who eventually became much better known for *Rebecca of Sunnybrook Farm*. Wiggin invited readers to *Timothy's Quest* with the rather lethargic salutation, "A story for anybody, young or old, who cares to read it." The book suggested that the secret of life was to know your "Mother, Nature, and . . . Father, God" and your "brothers, and sisters, the children of the world." Wiggin advocated being friendly and obeying the Ten Commandments. No wonder she was popular in the church-based library. However, the story mainly was about the noble, half-humorous attempts of a pre-teen boy named Timmy to find a mother for a motherless baby, knocking on doors and surprising the person who answered with, "Do you need any babies here, if you please?"

Unlike some young ladies her age, Sylvia was "Not very nervous; rather well balanced," according to a doctor's examination. She suffered from headaches occasionally, maybe because she was a little nearsighted, but she was very attractive, standing 5'4" and weighing 120 pounds by the time she had grown to young womanhood.

Sylvia aspired to an education, but where would the money come from to pay for it? In fact, where would anyone find a full-blown high school in Glenshaw? Since you couldn't find any such thing in town, Sylvia turned, as Alice had already done, to Park Academy, the high school branch of Park College in Parkville, Missouri, ten miles north of Kansas City. The Presbyterian school allowed students to work off tuition through a work-study type of program. It also offered the religious bent that Sylvia sought and her family approved. She said she wanted an education "To obtain a christian training so I may be more useful in the master's work."

PARK ACADEMY WAS A good arrangement for Sylvia and for the Harbaughs in general; not only were Alice and Sylvia there together, but Beatrice followed them to Park, and Milton graduated from there in 1911. Chambers

Harbaugh did not make enough money as a clerk to keep all those children in school, especially in an era when it was not an imperative for girls to go to school. In fact, on Sylvia's application to the Academy, the form asked, "Can you pay $75 or $60 per annum" ($1,938 or $1,550 today) in tuition, and she answered frankly, "No—I cannot." Park Academy's work-study arrangement truly was a godsend, therefore, for a set of forward-thinking parents from Glenshaw who wanted their son—*and* their daughters—educated.

By the time Sylvia graduated from the high school-level Park Academy, she had wholeheartedly embraced the women's liberation of her era that encouraged girls to have an education and a job. Of course, girls at Park Academy almost always thought of a college education as a possibility—right there was Park College, offering an appealing, Christly, coed education, and you could go even if you didn't have a lot of money. That's what Sylvia planned to do. As she had done in high school, Sylvia would work her way through Park College without her parents having to turn over their entire living to the school. Thus, she did not have to go far to continue seeking usefulness in the Master's work. One day she would flee the Master's work on the *Titanic*, but for now, she grew into adulthood in familiar surroundings.

# 2

# As Far From the Sea
# as a Person Could Get

Albert arrived at Park Academy in 1904, a good-looking kid with light hair and olive eyes. Slim of build, he was 5'10" and weighed 148 pounds. Stella came with him. Curiously, the Caldwell children entered the high school branch of Park, despite their rigorous high school preparation and their high school diplomas in hand. This probably disappointed both, as they had applied as college freshmen.

The school had been founded thirty years before as "Park College for Training Christian Workers" by George S. Park and Dr. John A. McAfee. The Reverend Elisha B. Sherwood, who had founded the Breckenridge church that William Caldwell now pastored, had had a hand in establishing Park College. While "I found the way clear and organized a Presbyterian church" in Breckenridge, Sherwood said, there was a severe lack of trained preachers fit or willing to lead congregations on the Missouri frontier. He recalled one preacher's unfortunate experience: "The first Sabbath he preached in a newly organized church. Some roughs came in and undertook to run the town. The citizens objected and the roughs began shooting, which brought on a bad state for the Sabbath day . . . He packed his grip the next morning and left."

Sherwood had to recruit pastors from New York, and they were often frustrated by the frontier nature of early Missouri. As a result, he said, "I became thoroughly convinced that our only hope of a supply of ministers and Christian workers was to start a college for training them on the field they are to occupy." In other words, the frontier of the United States needed a *lot* of spiritual help. George S. Park had offered the Presbyterian church a hotel building to be turned into a school for teaching ministers and Christian workers, but the idea didn't germinate until Sherwood met

*Mackay Hall, Park College's signature building, was photographed here by Albert, who kept the photo all his life. The building is still the centerpiece of the Park University campus.*

McAfee, a Missouri pastor who agreed with Sherwood on the need for a Christian college in Missouri. Sherwood introduced Park to McAfee, and Park College was born.

Not only did Park College recruit students from Presbyterian churches all over the nation, but it offered them a bargain education. Dr. McAfee developed a work program that allowed promising young Presbyterians to come to Park at a low cost; in fact, the *most* promising and *most* needy could attend without paying a penny. McAfee himself had not been wealthy as a youngster and sympathized with young people of similar background. He conceived of Park College as bringing students into a "well regulated Christian family. The name he gave it was, 'Park College Family,'" the Reverend Sherwood recalled. You had to be sixteen to join the "Family," but it was open to anyone who wanted a classical education and "who would honestly and faithfully manifest the disposition to use aright the opportunities afforded and would develop the capacity that promised usefulness in the church and the world." The Family in the high school arm was to act as a feeder to the college.

The first Family had seventeen students, but by 1893, there were 335. By 1905, the college hosted Presbyterian students from around the world, including locations as exotic as Syria and Bulgaria, alongside more familiar foreign locations such as Germany and Canada. Park graduates often mirrored the international flair of the college by going into missionary work all over the globe. By 1893, the Reverend Sherwood could boast, "Our students are in demand for the home and foreign mission work."

Albert and Stella could go to school because of the Family system. True, they did have to pay a little, but they got a real deal. Students started in "Family No. 2" or "Family No. 3," based on financial need. By paying $75 ($1,938 today) to join Family 2, Albert and Stella got to go home at the end of the school term. Students in Family 2 *could* start out paying just $60 ($1,550 today), but they had to stay into the summer to work, taking a shorter vacation. Albert and Stella had to furnish their own books (which could be rented from the library) and clothing and pillow and blanket. If they did well in school and couldn't afford to pay further, they moved up to Family No. 1, where textbooks and clothing were free. Family No. 3 was for people who were too poor to enter Family 2; they had a harder workload of half a day, rather than three hours a day for those in Family 2. No matter the work, Albert and Stella—and Sylvia—were well aware that their education was high quality but low price.

Park was pretty far from Sylvia's home in Glenshaw, but before she finished school her parents moved a little closer, to Colorado Springs, where their house at 321 Bijou Street featured a magnificent view of the mountains. Despite being away from home, Sylvia loved her school experience, throwing herself into various clubs and activities. Stella didn't like it; by 1906, she was apparently back at home in Breckenridge, paying taxes on her inherited jewelry and figuring out her future. She eventually moved on to Western College in Oxford, Ohio, but dropped out after a year.

Sylvia was undaunted when her dormitory, Park Hall, burned on February 25, 1901. After the flames were doused, Sylvia and the other residents of the Park Hall Family climbed on the ruins to pose for a picture. Among them was Sylvia's sister Alice, who also lived in the ill-fated dorm. Luckily there was time to save a good deal of the students' belongings, and Sylvia and Alice and the other girls moved to Barrett Hall. Sylvia was not discouraged by the fire, nor were the Harbaughs in general, as Beatrice and Milton followed Alice and Sylvia to Park. In fact, the presence of Beatrice and Milton

*Sylvia's dormitory in her high school years at Park Academy, Park Hall,
burned in 1901. Here she and other residents climb on the ruins. Sylvia
is the girl farthest to the left in the picture, and her older sister Alice is the
right-hand girl of the pair in the foreground nearest the camera, behind
the bricks.*

caused one of her professors to describe Sylvia as "Careful—Has had the
care and general oversight of a younger brother and sister." Sylvia's professor
also described her as agreeable and energetic —something of a dynamo.
Another professor described her as "very charming."

A YEAR AFTER THE dormitory fire, Sylvia had another big scare. She came
down with diphtheria in 1902, a potentially deadly disease. Her doctor
commented seven years later that she was still suffering from a weak throat
related to the diphtheria, but if so, Sylvia bulled her way through it to a
college career that included both singing and performing. By the time she

left college, in fact, she was known as an excellent "declaimer," or speaker, and she sang alto in various groups. Clearly, it would take more than diphtheria to keep Sylvia Harbaugh down. Despite the fire and the diphtheria, Sylvia completed her Academy training and qualified to attend Park College.

Both she and Albert continued in the Family work program in college. Albert's tasks included milking the school's cows. He also worked in a store and in the school's fundraising office, a job he would be a natural at, thanks to his extroverted personality. Albert also kept busy as a janitor in the much-used school chapel. In that job he pumped the organ for church services and various student assemblies. Students went to two Bible studies each weekday. They also read daily from the Bible (covering the entire book in a year), and following good Presbyterian practice, there was no silliness on Sunday. Students went to *five* Bible studies every Sunday. In fact, there were no classes on Mondays so that students would not be tempted to do homework or secular studying on the Sabbath. Presumably on those Mondays off, Albert cleaned up the chapel after all the Sunday traffic.

*The Class of 1909, Park College, posing as freshmen in 1905. Albert is in the upper left corner. Sylvia is diagonally below on the next row, directly below the girl with the white pom-pom dangling from her hat.*

Sherwood Girls ~ On the Ruins of Sherwood Home.
Destroyed by Fire, April 24, 1907.

*Not again! Sylvia's second dormitory fire at Park College left her momentarily homeless in 1907. Again, she climbed on the ruins, this time of Sherwood Home. She is in the second row, third from right.*

Sylvia probably worked in a kitchen or office. If she worked in the kitchen, she may have had to flee on April 24, 1907, when a fire broke out in the one-story dining room that adjoined the Sherwood Home. And then Sherwood Home—her dormitory—itself caught fire. Luckily, no one was hurt, although once again, Sylvia's residence lay in ashes. Once more there had been time to save most of the students' possessions. A faulty flue was at fault, causing $7,000 ($170,392 today) in losses (alas, the building was only insured for $3,000 ($73,025 today)). A high wind was gusting that morning, which blew embers onto the college granary. That building burned, too, while students and community members leaped to save barns and outbuildings. Since Albert worked on the college farm, he was perhaps among the worried people battling the flames.

This time Sylvia had to move to the home of a local family, that of G. M. Johnston, who took her in for six months. She made a good impression. "Silvia Harbaugh is a girl we know well and think a great deal of," Johnston wrote two years later when she graduated. "We regard her as one of the choicest girls in the present senior class of Park College."

Firefighting aside, Sylvia and Albert each worked at their Family jobs between three and five hours a day around their class schedules. He reported studying three to four hours a night, punctuated by the occasional tennis game. He sprained his ankle once, perhaps playing tennis, and hobbled in to Dr. J. H. Winter to patch it up. Meanwhile, Sylvia put in four or five hours a day studying. Although most professors thought of Sylvia as above average in intellect, one noted that she was not a brilliant scholar. Among other courses, Sylvia and Albert took trigonometry, Greek, Latin, English, and Bible. Sylvia had six years of Greek and got very good at it, tutoring others in the ancient tongue. She had five years of Latin and one of German. Albert likewise had a year of German and a lot of Greek and Latin, although he preferred Latin.

**Sylvia and Albert, like** all students, were expected to take part in public performances—oratory, singing, drama, concerts. That was easy. Performing was natural to both. Albert joined the College Glee Club, where he sang as the leading second tenor. He was so good that he was chosen as one of the members of the prestigious College Quartet, a gig that took him as a performer across the Midwest. Sylvia was also in two glee clubs and a choir at the college. Both she and Albert were members of the Parchevard-Calliopean literary society, Albert in the all-male Parchevard, and Sylvia in the women's Calliopean. The clubs socialized as well as sponsored scholarly events. Albert played the double bass in the school orchestra, but not well enough to brag about. Sylvia could pick out tunes on the organ and piano, but she was *really* good at the mandolin. Sylvia also stood out as a campus actress. One review noted that she always showed "grace and dignity on the stage."

Both Sylvia and Albert were members of Parkville Presbyterian Church by the time they were seniors in college. Sylvia taught a class of high school-aged boys in Sunday School and had much success turning their thoughts to God and their interest to their future in Christ. However, she was not a holier-than-thou goody-goody. She was popular among the students, according to one of her professors.

Park College Glee Club

*Top: The 1906 Park College Glee Club featured Albert, top row, second from right. He was a noted tenor. Bottom: Sylvia, second from right, was a good singer. She sang alto in this group, the Calliopean Glee Club.*

One thing Sylvia and Albert did together was to perform in the cast of the Parchevard-Calliopean 1908 production of Shakespeare's *The Winter's Tale*. Albert played the Clown, and in that role he got to deliver some chilling lines about a shipwreck:

> I would you did but see how it chafes, how it rages,
> how it takes up the shore! but that's not the
> point. O, the most piteous cry of the poor souls!

sometimes to see 'em, and not to see 'em; now the
ship boring the moon with her main-mast, and anon
swallowed with yest and froth, as you'd thrust a
cork into a hogshead. . . .

. . . But to make an

end of the ship, to see how the sea flap-dragoned
it: but, first, how the poor souls roared,
and the sea mocked them . . .

Those would have been mysterious, otherworldly lines to the young man from the Midwest. In Missouri he was about as far from the sea as a person could get. Still, the image of the sea swallowing the ship in a cruel game of "flap-dragon"—and then mocking its victims—was enough to raise shivers. Flap-dragon was a dangerous drinking game in which the player tried to swallow flaming raisins floating in brandy. The image in the lines evoked a nightmarish scene of a ship ablaze, its victims crying heartbreakingly and fruitlessly for help as they were devoured. Albert could not realize how ominously the lines foreshadowed the *Titanic*.

Sylvia played the role of Hermione, Queen to Leontes. Her character was portrayed as devoted to her husband—albeit falsely accused of infidelity. On stage Hermione made clear, "I do confess I loved him as in honour he required, With such a kind of love as might become a lady like me . . ." Sylvia adored the stage and was a bit of a drama queen in real life, too, according a fellow student who didn't much like her. And unlike Albert's lines about the shipwreck, which were just so much poetry that had no real bearing on his Midwestern life, Sylvia's words of commitment and devotion rang close to her heart.

ALTHOUGH SYLVIA'S HERMIONE WAS not in love with Albert's Clown in *The Winter's Tale,* Sylvia and Albert were no doubt romancing backstage. By then the two self-confident kids were starry-eyed for each other, and they were seriously discussing making a life together. Graduation loomed, and they had some careful planning to do to get their future in order. They were at the Park College for Training Christian Workers, and it seemed logical that Christian work would be their career choice. In fact, Sylvia had figured for the past five years that she would do missionary work when she finished school. Her cousins, George McCune and Miss Katherine McCune, were already in foreign missionary work. Even Sylvia's younger sister Beatrice, who somehow had graduated before Sylvia in 1908, was in Honolulu, Hawaii, where she was a teacher at a church-sponsored school. Missionary work was one field where women could take leadership roles, and Sylvia could picture herself doing that.

In the end, their future practically fell into Albert's lap. The plan to take missionary jobs in Siam began unfolding just after New Year's of their senior year, a time when almost every senior starts worrying about a job. Still, Albert didn't think he was shopping for a job overseas. As he described it, "There was a missionary, home on furlough, looking for a young fellow to go out to teach in a Presbyterian boys' school in Bangkok. The plan was to be there for seven years, learn the language, get on with the running of the school." The first seven years would be, essentially, an apprenticeship in the principal's role at the missionary school. After that the apprentice would go home on furlough for a year and then go back and take over the school permanently. The missionary doing the recruiting at Park was Dr. Eugene Dunlap, who spun a good tale as he tried to recruit some of the idealistic young men and women at Park. He reported colorfully that he and his wife had traveled around Siam on steamers, elephants, buffalo carts, and canoes.

To Albert's surprise, Park College President Lowell M. McAfee advised that he should consider the job that Dunlap was pitching. Albert was flattered. He spoke to Dr. Dunlap for an hour and a half about the position in Bangkok and then started up a correspondence with him. "I have intended to make teaching my life work, but had not thought seriously of the work in the Foreign field, before my conversation with Dr. Dunlap," Albert confessed later to the Presbyterian Foreign Missions Board. Albert consulted with his parents, who agreed with some reluctance that he could go. He also talked to church elders and to another foreign missionary about the job. And of course he conferred with Sylvia, who had been hoping to follow her cousins into missionary work anyway, and whose parents consented to her desire to join Albert in teaching overseas. Perhaps her career goals influenced Albert; women's career choices were somewhat limited, after all. As one newspaper put it after the *Titanic* wreck, "He did not believe he ought to take his bride to such a country," but Sylvia had set him straight: " . . . she said she could and would go if he did." Albert decided he wanted the job. There was a lot of appeal in following in the footsteps of his father in doing God's work, albeit in the role of a missionary teacher and not as a pastor. And Sylvia would be there alongside him.

In fact, Sylvia already had a connection to Siam. The well-known Bangkok missionary Edna Cole had come to campus with "a young lady from Siam," as Sylvia described her, in 1904. Truthfully, the young lady, Beatrice Moller, was an English-speaking girl who helped Miss Cole at the girls' Wang Lang School in Bangkok. However, Sylvia thought Beatrice needed help fitting into the American scene. As Sylvia put it, "I have been closely associated with her in helping her understand our American ways." Apparently Beatrice reciprocated. Sylvia rather naively felt better prepared for mission work in Siam as a result.

Albert, who had described himself as a somewhat nervous person but who had been described by someone else as having a personality that was "commanding, rather," was, indeed, both nervous and rather commanding as he planned for his career. He and Sylvia would graduate on June 24, 1909, and he let Presbyterian officials know he didn't expect a single day to go by before he started a job. He and his intended could sail for Bangkok the day after graduation, he insisted, forgetting that perhaps it might be nice to get married before they left. The job, he had heard, paid $625 per year ($15,214 today) for a single man, plus residence and transportation. If he were married, his salary would be a generous $1,250 (now $30,428) plus residence and transportation. When you counted in the house and transportation, it was more than twice what the average Presbyterian pastor made in the United States. Albert hoped his salary would include transportation for Sylvia as well. He anxiously asked for confirmation that her trip to Siam and back would be included in the pay. He told a key official that it was critical that his fiancee go with him, saying, "I thought at first

Albert F. Caldwell, '09
Bangkok, Siam.
Commissioned, '09. Returned Spring, '12

*A handsome fellow: Albert's college senior picture of 1909, with
information about his missionary service added later.*

*Mrs. Sylvia Harbaugh Caldwell, '09*
*Bangkok, Siam.*
*Commissioned, '09.    Returned, '12.*

*One of the prettiest girls from Colorado (as a newspaper called her after the* Titanic*): Sylvia's 1909 college senior picture, with information about her missionary service added later.*

of going alone but the girl whom I have for a long time intended to marry, expressed her willingness to go. I am sure I can do better work by having her with me." He added as a prophetic afterthought, "Of course we do not expect the missionary life to be an easy one."

Albert expected an immediate reaction to his application from the Foreign Missions Board. Instead, he played a fidgety waiting game. He groused to Stanley White of the Board, "I am turning down good positions, every few days now, so am anxious to hear, what the result of the Action of the Board will be."

White was alarmed to hear about the jobs Albert turned down. He warned, "I would also say that the position you have in mind, at the Christian Boys High School is one that needs not only head knowledge but experience in teaching and managing a school." Albert had the former but not the latter, and White was hinting pointedly that Albert should look elsewhere.

Dr. McAfee did his best to quell any worries the Foreign Missions Board had about Albert's lack of teaching experience. McAfee recommended Albert for the job with ringing words: "We have found him a fine student, a man of refinement, a leader among his fellows, bright and cheery in his work . . . He has not taught before but I think him possessed of those latent qualities that will develop in a satisfactory manner . . . the Board makes no mistake if he be accepted for the position."

Albert's anxiety over the job only increased. He noted crossly to White, "As it is now, I go to the Post Office every mail with the hopes of hearing your final decision . . . I know I am very impatient and if only myself were concerned I would not care so much." The exasperated White replied, "I would call your attention to the fact that it is barely a month since your application . . . and that it is a very hazardous thing to be over-precipitate in determining a man's life work." White advised him to interview again with Dr. Dunlap, which Albert did.

White reported a positive reaction from Dunlap on May 20, 1909, and not only told Albert and Sylvia the good news, but insisted they come to New York to a conference for outgoing missionaries. The conference would take place in June, with the Presbyterian church paying their expenses to New York, including transportation and entertainment. Albert and Sylvia could take the train round trip from Kansas City for $40 ($974 today), a dazzling sum for students who couldn't afford regular college tuition. The ticket price showed the future missionaries how key it was for the Board of Foreign Missions to pay their travel to and from assignments around the world. They would ultimately be haunted by the Board's stranglehold on travel funding, but of course they had no inkling of that yet.

Despite the church having paid such a pretty penny for tickets, Sylvia and Albert's train was delayed and they missed a connection. They had to send a telegram from Detroit, explaining their late arrival.

One goal of theirs in New York was to purchase an "outfit" for Siam—the household goods and specialty clothing they would need. The Presbyterians allotted $400 ($9,737 in today's dollars) for such. Albert worried whether that amount would be sufficient, and he was assured that the church did not intend to send them into the field unprepared. A missionary to Melanesia, not all that far from Siam, suggested that missionary schoolteachers take table, chairs, bed, a deck chair, blankets, sheets (you'd *only* need a sheet to sleep under, he assured), a heavy covering in case of fever, a tub and soap for washing, irons, canteens, dinnerware, can opener, corkscrew, cookware, stove, lamps or candles, cool underwear (*no* flannel), a belt that would protect the stomach (to ward off disease), raincoat, *lots* of boots (they wore out quickly), straw hats, spats for ladies (to protect their ankles from mosquitoes), and the all-critical mosquito net, which meant you needed to bring needles and thread to repair the net immediately as needed. Shorts and short sleeves were okay, too. Presumably while Albert and Sylvia were in New York, they purchased and arranged for shipping their outfit to Siam, as Dr. Dunlap had suggested, because goods and freight were cheaper from New York. Sylvia perhaps dropped down to Washington, D.C., on this trip, on a specialized missionary task of her own: she would represent Washington-area Presbyterian churches in their fundraising for the Jane Hays Memorial Fund, which aimed to build a new girls' school in Bangkok.

Even after the big trip to New York, there were still hitches. Here Albert was with a job in hand, when it was almost snatched from his grasp. Dr. McAfee happened to run into White and mentioned Albert's name. White's reply caused a crisis, and he got a chewing out from Albert, who wrote to him, "President McAfee gave me quite a scare . . . He said that he had been in your office and you had informed him that another man named Conybeare had applied for the same position" and that Conybeare would likely get it. McAfee apparently turned in a panic to Dunlap, who assured him that Conybeare was applying for another job, "the Y.M.C.A. work." Well, that was a relief, but Albert wrote to White, just to be sure.

The Bangkok job *was* sure, and he and Sylvia were formally appointed on June 7, 1909. As the icing on the cake, the newly minted missionaries had a companion heading to Siam. A Park College classmate, Ed Spilman, was going over to Bangkok, too, to work for the American Presbyterian Press.

What Albert and Sylvia didn't know, as they prepared for their life together in Siam, was that Professor M. C. Findlay of Park College had done his best to discourage the Board of Foreign Missions from taking Sylvia. His comments reflected an interesting mix of admiration for Sylvia and disdain for the missionary scene, which was out of control, as he saw it. A Park graduate, Victoria McArthur, had nearly worked herself to death in India, and she was now home for some badly needed rest and relaxation. Findlay did not like what he saw of poor Victoria, and he hoped fervently as a result that Sylvia would *not* go abroad. He wrote on Sylvia's recommendation form:

> I do not believe Miss Harbaugh is well fitted for a frontier life and some of the physical hardships required of some missionaries. I do not believe her health although good for the average young woman, will stand what Miss Victoria McArthur and others like her have gone through. I am getting more and more of the opinion that some of the work expected of the missionaries is impossible. Some of the missionaries long in the field have become so pigheaded and bossy that it is almost impossible for the new missionary . . . to work with them and maintain their self respect. Miss Harbaugh is able, agreeable and cultured and I should hate to see her sent to some fields, which might be mentioned. In the right place she will do well.

The fact that Findlay was a biology professor may have given his assessment of Sylvia's stamina and health even more credibility.

Another reference for Sylvia hinted at a little doubt as to her readiness for the religious part of mission life. G. M. Johnston commented, "The active vital Christian Character which comes with the experience of deepest need and the abundant supply of God's Grace—she has not yet received." However, he heartily recommended her, expecting her to progress quickly. He added, "I think there will be no mistake in her appointment."

Sylvia and Albert were blissfully unaware of these foreboding assessments of Sylvia. They only knew they were due to leave for Siam in September.

But first there were the matters of graduating and getting married, which almost seemed anticlimactic against the bright horizon of the future. They graduated with A.B. degrees on June 24 —Albert graduated with honors and gave an honors oration at graduation. They spent the time between their graduation and the end of August planning their wedding a little and their move to Siam a lot. The wedding was held at Chambers and Sylvia Harbaugh's home in Colorado Springs on September 1, 1909, with the beautiful mountains looming just over the brow of the hill of Bijou Street. Albert's father came over from Missouri to officiate; he was now the pastor at the Presbyterian church in Marceline. Thirty-five witnesses were on hand.

THE NEWLYWEDS SET OUT for Siam the very day of their wedding. Although it seemed like an idyllic start to an equal partnership, it could not have been a good way to start a marriage. No doubt the journey to their ship, leaving from San Francisco, counted as a honeymoon, but after a mere week as a married couple, they found themselves aboard the *Manchuria*, set to sail the Pacific. Albert celebrated his twenty-fourth birthday on the day they left America for Siam, making their farewell to the United States all the more significant. Somewhere back in the Midwest, Stella turned twenty-three and was in love herself and would shortly marry. She had come back to Missouri from Ohio and was now planning to wed J. E. Plummer, a former bookkeeper at the local bank who had recently become a "frank-spoken, genial" lawyer. A piece of childhood died that September 8 for the twinlike duo. Married life lay ahead. For Albert and Sylvia, marriage brought them to a sheer cliff of change. According to their career plans, they'd never really live in America again.

The *Manchuria* tried hard to be a luxury ship, bragging in its brochure that it was the steadiest boat on the Pacific. Its construction, the ad went, "assures freedom from seasickness." Alas, the advertisement was wishful thinking. During the long, long crossing of nearly six weeks, Sylvia was seasick. Landlubbers from the Midwest, she and Albert were not used to boats or the sea, as they found out most unpleasantly.

If it hadn't been for the uncomfortable nature of the voyage, the trip would have been a true excitement to young people from poor backgrounds who wanted to see—and save—the world. "We went out by way of the Hawaiian Islands, Japan, and China, and round past what is now Vietnam and up the Gulf of Siam, and 20 miles up the river to Bangkok," Albert recalled more than sixty years later, the trip still as clear in his memory as though he had just taken it. On the way they saw cities they could not have imagined as they milked cows and cleaned kitchens at Park: Honolulu, Hawaii (perhaps they managed a visit with Beatrice, who told everyone the place was a paradise ); Yokohama, Kobe, and Nagasaki in a rapidly modernizing Japan; the Chinese trading city of Shanghai; and the British outpost of Hong Kong. They finally arrived in Bangkok, Siam, on October 16, many weeks and a world away from where they had begun. It had been an interesting trip, and Asia was already fascinating. But most of all, Sylvia was relieved to make solid land again.

# 3

# Caught in a Maelstrom

Bangkok was enchanting, not just because at last Sylvia could eat dinner without fear of losing it, but also because it was a point of contact between two vastly different cultures. Albert described Bangkok poetically as "that Oriental city where Eastern and Western civilization exist side by side." Tourists rarely made it all the way to Bangkok, so it was exotic and untouched, while also—thanks to a liberal, Western-minded king—open-minded when it came to missionaries. The city, which was Siam's capital, was bisected by the Chao Phraya River and was flat as a sheet of paper, punctuated only by one artificial hill and one tall pagoda. There were lots of canals that had once been used for transport. Now, however, there was an "almost incredible" number of automobiles jockeying with bicycles, carriages, and rickshaws on the seventy-five miles of roads. There were even twenty miles of electric tramways through the city, "and airships have been advertised," one report said, although the writer had not seen one. The city boasted other modern amenities such as electric lights and picture shows. The year the Caldwells arrived, Bangkok had 628,675 residents in the city proper. The metro area was home to a colorful array of people, including the majority Siamese, but also a large number of Chinese, a noticeable number of Indians and Malays, a smattering of Europeans and Americans, and a bunch of Christian missionaries busying themselves in doing good.

For a while, the Caldwells loved Siam. They found their work "exceedingly interesting" and thought the country was delightful. Albert wrote to the *Park College Stylus*, "The climate here seems to agree with us and we have never felt better in our lives. Since the first of November the weather has been ideal. Bangkok is quite a modern city for the Orient and we were agreeably surprised. The king is enthusiastic for the progress of Siam." In the Caldwells' eyes, Bangkok spread out as their own personal canvas, and they tried to paint the life they had led onto it. Albert organized a glee club, and by June of 1910, the club was performing all around the city. Sylvia also performed in Bangkok, apparently giving dramatic recitations. As a fellow missionary noted after one of their performances, the Caldwells "made quite a hit."

The newlyweds lived on the top floor above the chapel of the school where both taught. Their living quarters featured a deep veranda and balcony. Verandas were vital in a place blasted by the tropical sun and dripping in sweltering humidity. "We do most of our living on the verandas, following from one side to the other as the sun makes moving necessary," Daisy Spilman, Ed's wife, wrote after she arrived in Siam a few years later. If the Caldwell home was anything like the Spilmans', there were five rooms, four of them fifteen feet square, and all opening into the large middle room of fifteen by thirty feet. All windows functioned as doors and consequently were seven feet high. Over those were transoms of three feet. You could let in a lot of air if you needed to, and certainly you'd need to . . . but unfortunately, you also let in mosquitoes. Daisy complained, "Life is worth living here, and would be very pleasant were it not for the mosquitoes, which are here in thousands. In one room we have a mosquito house. Something like you screen in a porch. Everyone here natives and all sleep under mosquito nets." The Spilman home featured a kitchen and two bathrooms, with one bathroom perhaps designated for servants. "We have a cook, table and house boy, and a wash lady," Daisy reported. "Occasionally we hire an extra coolie for yard work but he is not on the regular pay roll." Albert and Sylvia also had a cook, whose illness one evening meant they had to cancel a dinner party. No doubt the Caldwells also had a household servant and a wash lady, as the Spilmans did. And the Caldwells suffered with mosquitoes, too. Once they had guests who reported they didn't sleep well, so Sylvia spent a great deal of effort trying to kill mosquitoes to make everyone more comfortable.

Another missionary the Caldwells soon met was Samuel Conybeare, the man who had unknowingly given Albert such a scare back in June when it appeared he had snatched the Bangkok schoolteaching job from under Albert's nose. Conybeare was organizing a YMCA-related project to help the Siamese understand business practices. Sylvia and Albert, along with Ed

Spilman, met Sam and Bess Conybeare when they arrived, in the pouring rain, in Bangkok. As it turned out, Albert and Sylvia came to like Conybeare and his wife very well—although ultimately it would take the wreck of the *Titanic* to undo the damage unintentionally done by Conybeare. But that was in the future, after things went sour in Siam. For now, Sylvia and Albert found a lot in common with the Conybeares. The couples spent a lot of time together, enjoying such pastimes as singing to the mandolin and playing dominoes. They were tourists in Bangkok, too, attending illuminations over the river and finding a good view of the palace, and once Sam and Albert went to see an "aeroplane." They took pictures of the airplane, which they developed themselves. The Conybeares and Caldwells particularly liked playing card games such as Forty-Two, Flinch, and Somerset, and Bess often reported in her diary that they "had a jolly time." In honor of Sylvia's birthday in 1910, they played billiards and Forty-Two and had dinner together, a "very happy day," Bess recorded.

OF COURSE, THE MISSIONARIES worked hard at their jobs, too, and the Caldwells seemed to like theirs. Other missionaries reported that Albert and Sylvia had a "zest for the work." It was a good thing they had a lot of zest. When the young couple arrived, Bangkok Christian College—then

*The Caldwells lived on the top floor above the chapel at Bangkok Christian College. Albert might be the figure on the balcony in this shot, taken by his friend Sam Conybeare.*

known as Bangkok Boys' High School—was in the midst of a key change. Not only was Albert being groomed as the future principal, but the school was undergoing transformation in name from a high school into a college. That didn't mean the school taught college men. Its students ranged from small boys to high-schoolers, but it was a school with large numbers and wide influence, and such schools were called colleges in the Orient. "From the Siamese standpoint it is now in fact a college. True it is not as far advanced as the usual college at home, but we must look at it from the standpoint of other Mission colleges and so-called Siamese Colleges here in Bangkok," Siam missionary R. C. Jones explained to the Foreign Missions Board back in New York. "It makes us feel decidedly left [behind] to see some of the reports of Educational work sent out from time to time in which schools, far lower than ours, are rated far above it because of its name. Call it 'The Bangkok Christian College' and be done with the naming of it."

Albert taught English at Bangkok Christian College, among other duties, and Sylvia taught alongside him, surely a pleasing circumstance for newlyweds. Albert told the *Park College Stylus* that his students were learning fast. "All the boys speak more or less English," he said.

Part of Albert's job was to work with Sam Conybeare in the Boon Itt Memorial Institute, the YMCA venture that was Conybeare's pet project. The institute on Worachak Road was a grand recycling project in a highly favored neighborhood: the Presbyterians took over an old building and rehabbed it for community outreach. Sylvia and Albert were on the committee in charge of furnishing it, no small task. When they were done, the institute featured an assembly hall that could seat several hundred people, a library and its related reading room, an area for games and socializing, a dining area "which can be used for light gymnastic work as well," a guest room, kitchen, locker room, and bath area. Outside there were courts for Albert's favorite game—tennis—and badminton. Boon Itt Memorial was described as "an integral part of the Mission's effort to reach the young men that have graduated from our schools and the many others who have flocked to the metropolis from the smaller cities." A lot of young men hung out in the game rooms, and Boon Itt threw socials for them. On the more serious side, the institute's personnel held church services and gave lectures illustrated by stereopticon slides. The institute offered classes in English, French, and music. Conybeare, Albert, and Dr. Wachter worked together on these classes, with Albert apparently teaching music. The new Institute garnered lots of optimism among Presbyterians. As a publication of the day put it, "The possibilities of the Institute are unbounded."

It took broad-mindedness to run institutions such as Boon Itt and the Christian College. Principal-in-training Albert had 160 to 200 students to

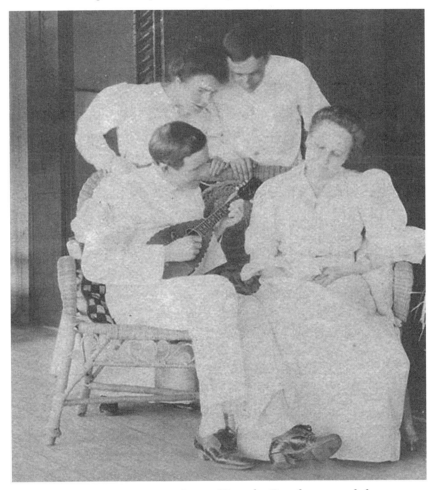

*Music was a great pastime in Siam. Here the Conybeares and the Caldwells enjoy singing to the mandolin. Sylvia was quite good on the mandolin. In this picture it appears a balding Albert could play it, too.*

mind in the college depending on the year, and only a small number professed Christianity. The majority seemed to believe, but "are perhaps held back from confessing Christ by the pressure of Buddhist friends and their heathen environment," one account reported. "As evidence of this Christian spirit, they have refused the past year to take part in athletic contests with the national schools because the games were played on the Sabbath day." The writer admitted, "It is only fair to say, however, that they may have acted partly upon the knowledge that the college would not permit Sunday games."

Albert's young men were destined for important roles in government, and although many weren't wholly converts, they were friendly to Christianity and to missionaries in general. There was *some* success in converting the young men. Kru Noi, an advanced student, progressed far enough to teach in another mission school. A Presbyterian Foreign Missions Board report showcased Kru Noi's success in its plea to Presbyterians to ante up more money to "increase [the college's] equipment and efficiency." Bangkok Christian College had five buildings on two and a half acres of land, but it needed a water supply, upgraded equipment, and "two or three expert teachers. It is absolutely essential to the life and growth of our mission schools that they keep ahead of the government schools." It would, the Foreign Missions Board warned, be shortsighted of churchmen to let the college lose its edge.

Albert found he had a tough act to follow. Leaders of the school, including the Reverend W. G. McClure and Dr. Wachter, had been wise managers, putting the school "in point of efficiency at the very top of all educational institutions in lower Siam." During the Caldwells' tenure, McClure and Wachter traded the principal's role. McClure's wife, Jeanie (a Park College graduate), helped run the school when her husband was in charge, as Mrs. Wachter did when *her* husband led the school. Miss Annabel Galt was a faithful teacher, and the Caldwells were also on the faculty. There was a handful of native teachers. "The whole spirit and atmosphere of the College is Christian," one observer wrote. "The educational work is always kept subordinate to the spiritual and evangelistic. There is no stronger missionary agency in Siam than Bangkok Christian College." In fact, the college was nearly self-supporting.

*A large Bangkok family gathers for a wedding in or shortly after the Caldwells' era in Siam. The bride, on the left, had just arrived from China to marry the very tall young man.*

Yes, it would be hard to fill the principal's shoes, but Albert was eager to try. He started studying the Siamese language. It was so different from the Latin, Greek, and German he had studied! He mulled over grammar lessons, perhaps from a book published by the American Missionary Press at Bangkok, *An Elementary Handbook of the Siamese Language.* The *Handbook* explained, "The Siamese language belongs to the class of 'Toned' languages . . . There is no greater error than to suppose that these tones are of slight importance. They are the most vital point and the whole *crux* of the Siamese language." Ironically, the book warned that it was nearly impossible to learn these tones from a book. *An Elementary Handbook* recommended earnestly that the reader get a local to help teach him the language. Albert probably did just that, and he discovered right away that the people there most certainly did *not* call the place "Siam," but instead called it "Muang Thai." "Muang" was the word for "land," and "Thai" meant "free," he found out. Thus, "Muang Thai" was "Thailand," the land of the free. "They put the adjective after the noun," he explained.

**DELIGHTFULLY FOR THE CALDWELLS** and Ed Spilman, there were a number of Park College alumni in Siam. On November 24, 1910, alums got together for a dinner in Bangkok. Ed wrote to the alumni magazine about it. He did not give details on the menu, but he did comment in a playful letter home about the food that missionaries usually ate in Siam. "A missionary is still human even after he has left the shores of the U.S. and he or she still appreciates and enjoys good square meals," he said, hinting that they ate as near American style as was possible. But an American menu was not always possible. His wife remarked that they chiefly ate beef in roasts and "hamberg steaks." She complained, "The Chinese [merchants] do not know how to cut the meat so they chop it up and as a result we have to grind it. We tried some steaks but they were not a success except as a chewing bee." Otherwise, they ate "second class chickens and half sized eggs of questionable age," as Daisy Spilman called them. You could get any vegetable in Bangkok that you could get in the United States except celery—the missionaries missed it—and they were forced to cook their cabbage and lettuce. They had fresh peas and ears of corn year-round, and "green beans twice a day the year thru," Daisy said. Surely they got tired of green beans. Many vegetables, she noted, were imported from China but were still cheaper than at home. As to fruits—now there Siam was *truly* exotic. The Caldwells and everyone else could choose from four varieties of oranges and no less than twenty types of bananas. "Other fruits in abundance more than twice as many varieties than in America. And obtainable year round," Daisy Spilman reported. Food was cheap, she added.

Thus, in the November 1910 dinner for Park alums, the diners probably ate some form of beef, some exotic type of banana, corn, and the ever-present green beans. Ed noted in his article on the event, "Owing to illness, Mrs. Sylvia Harbaugh Caldwell, '09, was not present." The reason was a happy one, even if Sylvia did have to put up once again with annoying nausea: she was two months pregnant. Her baby was due the following June.

Albert got a kick out of children—as the older sibling to Stella and Vera, he always had. He loved photographing the funny Siamese children. He snapped a photo of one little boy running directly toward the camera, naked except for an ankle bracelet, a huge smile on his face. "This is how they dress in Siam!" he guffawed later when showing it off to his family. He enjoyed these nearly naked Siamese children and earnestly worked to urge them toward salvation and toward learning English. He and his colleagues also saw to it that the Siamese children had the kind of fun American children had at Christmas. He wrote:

> We have had Thanksgiving, Christmas and New Years, all without snow. Nevertheless the Season's spirit crept in, a little . . .
>
> On Christmas eve, following our custom, the Sunday school gave a Christmas entertainment. The school Chapel was appropriately decorated. The glad, good news was told in song and story. The little tots found a warm spot in the listeners' hearts, while the older boys set forth, in graver style, some thoughts that cluster around Christmas time.
>
> There were several special pieces of music, by the School "Glee Club" and a quartet, all of which were nicely sung. The entire program was in "English." Just at the close of the entertainment, Santa Claus arrived in a beautiful white boat, nicely decorated and filled with good things, which were distributed to those present.

The program was joyous, but daily work at the school was demanding. As Jeanie McClure reported, she and other teachers spent from 8:30 A.M. to 4 P.M. in the classroom, and once Sylvia complained to Bess Conybeare of her "awful life at H.S. stayed until 12:30" one night. After school ended each day, Jeanie McClure was called on to help supply music at Boon Itt, to receive visitors, to doctor the sick, and everyone else had similar extra duties. In 1910, the popular and respected King Chulalongkorn of Siam died after a reign of nearly forty-two years, causing extra work for the students and teachers at Bangkok Christian. The school truly wanted to honor the great king, who had abolished debt slavery, established post office and telegraph services, built railroads, and suppressed the widespread use of opium. "The whole country went into mourning for a year," explained teacher Annabel Galt.

The staff and students leaped into action. "Schools have been allowed to go to pay respects to the 'lying in state' of the body, of the late king," Albert reported. The king had been cremated and his remains were in an urn. But before they went to offer their sympathy at the urn, "the boys were drilled to move and march in a prescribed order," Albert said. "The Siam Electricity Co. gave us free use, of their tram cars, to convey the boys, to the Palace. In the name of the school, a beautiful wreath, of artificial flowers, was laid at the foot of the urn. This wreath was secured by voluntary cash contributions of the pupils of the school." Given academic lessons, performances, athletic events, drilling and marching, teaching English, collecting money, and chaperoning the solemn field trip, added to other duties at Boon Itt, teachers at Bangkok Christian were on their toes many hours in a day. They were weary. There were only six of them. An absent missionary teacher would be sorely missed.

And alas, by now Sylvia was absent a lot. She became pregnant in September 1910, and she pretty much did no work at the school throughout her pregnancy. School closed in mid-March and reopened again on May 1 after the teachers had a vacation during the hot season, but Sylvia did not rejoin them.

WHILE SYLVIA PLODDED THROUGH the long, fat, days of pregnancy in the excruciating heat of Siam, some dreadful things were happening in the mission. The Conybeares had been unhappy for some time, and Bess's diary bubbled with worry as things went wrong with the Boon Itt assignment. She and Sam were blue one day about it, and another day Bess said they were very discouraged. Two days later they were "all in a stew over Boon Itt matters." Soon the Conybeares were given a new assignment to a distant missionary station at Petchaburi. The Conybeares would not hear of it. They flatly refused to make the move. Mission officials wouldn't budge at first in a true staredown with the couple. By the time the officials blinked and told Conybeare he could stay on at Boon Itt if he liked, he and Bess refused that, too. They would prefer to go home. They were bold enough to speak to other missionaries about that, although their boss, F. L. Snyder, "wouldn't hear of us leaving. Dreadfully blue day—homesick all day," Bess wrote in her diary. Later Snyder apparently lost his temper and "Tells us to get out if we are going to." It wasn't that easy. The Conybeares had to send letters requesting to resign to the Board of Foreign Missions, while Snyder tried to change their minds. The Board remanded the request to the mission,

*At first Albert thought Sam Conybeare had stolen his job, but the families wound up as fast friends in Siam. From left, Albert, Sam, Sylvia, Bess.*

causing Bess to break into tears. Eventually officials stopped Conybeare's salary, because Conybeare insisted on resigning before his contract was up. One official doing battle with them said the Conybeares had focused hard on "the unpleasant things, real or imaginary, till they have worked themselves up into a morbid mental attitude."

During a heated exchange with mission officials in Bangkok, Conybeare blurted out that other missionaries were unhappy, too, not just him. Some discontented missionaries, he said, had been squirreling away money on the sly to flee the country before the Foreign Missions Board set them free on furlough. As R. C. Jones, chairman of the Siam mission's Executive Committee, described the incident, "Some statements were made by Mr. Conybeare when his case was before the Ex[ecutive] Com[mittee] to the effect that certain other missionaries were laying aside certain amounts every month in anticipation of going home," thus reneging on their contract. According to Jones, this statement "evidently" referred to the Caldwells. The Conybeares resigned after making a big scene (as Snyder saw it). The couple left for Singapore, where they would catch a vessel going home—they didn't care which direction, whether via Atlantic or Pacific, as long as it got them home. Snyder warned headquarters in New York that Conybeare intended to drag various missionaries' names through the mud in an attempt to convince the Foreign Missions Board to cancel the Board's financial claims against the couple. Until that time, the Conybeares would have to pay their own travel home. Bess, for her part, was elated to get official permission from the Foreign Missions Board to appeal the decision regarding the cancelled salary when they got to New York.

This fight was talked about all over the mission (a large number of the personnel commented on it in their correspondence), and the Caldwells knew all about it. The Conybeares' financial predicament, as they traveled home without a salary, was an obvious reminder of how costly a trip halfway around the world was. As Sylvia struggled through pregnancy, the Conybeares' battle could not have helped her growing feeling of being trapped.

Sylvia was by then spiraling into a long decline in her health. First there was the pregnancy—a first pregnancy, with its unfamiliar and frightening aches, pains, and discomforts. Add the unrelenting heat of the tropics, and Sylvia was miserable. Bess Conybeare, in fact, had noted in her diary day after day in the fall of 1910 that Sylvia was ill. Sylvia once even came to stay with Bess, who reported that Sylvia "sits long in chair—can't eat." A few days later Sylvia had gotten so sick that Bess had to call Albert to come. Sylvia's illness was so long and discouraging that shortly, as Bess wrote in her diary, "Caldwells determined to return to America, too." On another day, Bess noted, "Mr. C. worried about his wife," and another day she had recorded, "Mrs. C. not well—expects to go to Nursing Home." School closed for the hot season just as Sylvia neared the six-month mark in her pregnancy. By now she would have been roasting had she been pregnant at home in the United States, but *everyone*, pregnant or not, was roasting in Siam. Sylvia's misery was that much worse than anyone else's, compounded by the new life now kicking in her belly all through the agonizing hot season, which ran through the end of April. It was with joy and relief that she successfully brought baby Alden Gates Caldwell into the world on June 10, 1911, but a month later she was down with a fever. She "has been pretty well otherwise since the birth of their child," her boss, W. G. McClure, said, but he did take note of the fever.

ALBERT HAD SHAKEN THE family tree to find Alden's name. The baby was named for that almost mythical Caldwell family connection to the famous Pilgrim John Alden. The "Gates" was Fannie Caldwell's maiden name. Albert's grandfather Francis Gates had lived with the Caldwells when Albert was a child back in Missouri and in fact still lived with Albert's parents. Sylvia snapped a photo of Albert and little Alden. Albert, perched in an exotic wicker chair, mud on his boots from the mud streets, dressed in a light suit to ward off the tropical heat, made a googly face at the attentive newborn. Behind them the louvered doors to their house were open and a tropical plant grew nearby, both testimony to how hot Siam was. But never mind that. Albert wrote happily on the back of the photo, speaking for Alden,

*New daddy Albert makes a googly face at Alden outside their home in Bangkok, June or July 1911.*

"For the land of love is this my dad? He looks like a circus clown." Albert put the picture in the mail to the United States for the proud grandparents to see. He and Sylvia wrote home to the alumni magazine at Park College, announcing the birth of their son:

Is Alden Gates, Called Well?
Dear Friend, I arrived in Bangkok, safe and sound, Saturday morning, June 10, at eight o'clock. They think that I am going to have blue eyes. My hair is light and I weigh eight pounds. My mama is getting along nicely and my papa is so proud, he don't know what to do . . .

The goofy announcement finally ran when Alden was four months old, and the editor noted that the "interesting item has been misplaced and delayed so long and often, that we began to fear the boy would have whiskers before it got to print."

By the time the news of Alden's birth finally ran in the *Alumniad*, the door had slammed shut on Albert's career plans to take over the crown jewel of Siamese Christian schools. Through that dismal rainy season after Alden's birth, the Caldwells continued on in Bangkok, Albert enjoying his work but Sylvia struggling through the customary post-delivery confinement and then skipping school even after the confinement should have been over. She certainly wasn't pulling her weight in the mission, and she was probably worried that everyone's patience would wear thin. However, she was sure there was something horribly wrong with her. She had not coped well with pregnancy in the boiling tropics, and now she couldn't get her strength back nor go back to work. Her condition reflected the prophetic recommendation letter she never knew about from her professor, Dr. M. C. Findlay, who had worried that she would not be physically up to the frontier circumstances she might encounter as a missionary.

Other people in the mission had all sorts of ideas: she would feel better after the cool season. She should apply to transfer to a new station or leave for awhile and then come back. She should take a rest there in Siam and see how she felt. She would get over it. It was only pregnancy, and she just hadn't had any experience with pregnancy.

Sylvia had consulted a former missionary doctor still working in town, Dr. Carl C. Hansen. Everyone loved him because he didn't charge the missionaries a penny—or, in Siamese money, a tical. All Sylvia's friends went to Hansen and trusted him. When Dr. Charles C. Walker arrived back in the mission from furlough, Sylvia asked him to examine her as well. The news was not good. He diagnosed her as having a pathological case of neurasthenia, brought on by residence in the tropics.

There it was, the dread verdict: neurasthenia. It was the type of scary word Sylvia and Albert had been fearing. The disease is pretty much unknown today, except as a piece of medical history. It was popularly diagnosed from 1869 to 1932, but after that time it seemed to disappear from the diagnosis lexicon and its sufferers would by then generally be classed as having a psychiatric disorder, not a physical one. As medical historian Mike Flannery puts it today, "That's a diagnosis they gave when they didn't know what was wrong with you. It was ill-defined, a catch-all." To many in 1911, neurasthenia was related to hysteria and hypochondria. And yet, thousands of people with physical symptoms were diagnosed with neurasthenia every year during the heyday of the disease. One modern doctor suggests that people who were once told they had neurasthenia might be diagnosed today with maladies ranging from chronic fatigue syndrome to irritable bowel syndrome to panic attacks to fibromyalgia to dysautonomia. Another source believes that today's depression, postpartum depression, mononucleosis, and post-traumatic stress disorder might have at one time been called neurasthenia.

Physical symptoms of neurasthenia as listed by doctors of Sylvia's era varied, but all included, at their core, severe muscle weakness and fatigue. Patients reported assorted problems, such as extreme numbness in arms, legs, hands, or feet; trembling or aching legs and inability to walk more than a little way; constipation; severe chronic headaches; backaches; blurred or misty vision; shortness of breath; irritability; restlessness and insomnia.

Most disheartening of all in Sylvia's case was Dr. Walker's further comment in making his diagnosis. He was afraid, he said, that if Sylvia did not get out of the tropics and return to the United States, "she may lose her mind same as Mrs. Barrett of Nan Laos did . . . It would be bad to keep them on and have her run down and become an invalid for life." That was terrifying. The prediction of invalidism was bad enough, but the invocation of the Barrett case was worse. Mrs. A. P. Barrett, a missionary whom the Caldwells had heard a lot about, had gone to Laos full of high hopes in 1903 —but five years later she had completely broken down in the tropical climate. As an official church report explained, the mission in Nan, Laos, had a hard year in 1908. On "March 25 native boats took away Mr. and Mrs. David Park on account of the prolonged illness of Mrs. Park," the report ran. David Park had been the schoolmaster in Nan, so Mr. Barrett took over the school. Apparently the schoolboys were running wild. "He quickly got hold of the boys," the report said. "Admirable progress was being made and Mr. and Mrs. Barrett were beginning to find they had found their real place, when the calamity befell them that broke off their missionary careers and cast a gloom over the school." Mrs. Barrett had had her crisis. On "July 8 other boats carried away Mr. and Mrs. Barrett, and with a great load of sorrow in Mrs. Barrett's sufferings," the report mourned. The fact that the Barretts had been schoolteachers, too, probably didn't help the Caldwells' perception of the matter. Given the fact that the official report was probably sanitized to a great degree, the real-life story was likely far more dire. Dr. Walker didn't have to say another word past "Mrs. Barrett"; the Caldwells were thoroughly alarmed. If they got anything out of the story of Mrs. Barrett, it was a pattern for what to do about such an illness: get out of Siam before it was too late.

There was no choice, as the Caldwells saw it. Albert made an impassioned plea for understanding in a letter to Dr. Arthur Judson Brown of the Board of Foreign Missions as he and Sylvia sought official permission to leave their posts in Siam. He pointed out that they had "been ordered home" on account of Sylvia's health. He explained to Dr. Brown:

> It is with deep regret, that we must give up the work, which we have learned to love . . . But it seems that God has willed that we leave our work here and he has a place for us to serve our Master in the Home-land. All we can say is, "his will be done." We came to Siam, expecting to spend our lives here and it does seem discouraging to have to give up our work so soon. But we must not complain . . .

Mrs. Caldwell has been sick, from the day we arrived in Siam . . . She suffered a great deal during these past two years . . . But we were told that every one must first become acclimated. I myself have been in perfect health, and like the climate. Dr. Hansen told me some time ago, that we would eventually have to give up the work here, as Mrs. Caldwell could not stand the Tropics.

In so saying, he conveniently forgot or glossed over that Sylvia had really only become chronically ill when she became pregnant. No doubt his letter to Brown included a dose of exaggeration, whether on purpose or brought on by panic. Albert included a pitiful comment, that of a young husband who appeared to be worried sick that he personally had caused irrevocable damage: "I fear now that I should have brought her home sooner."

But something else was unwell, not just Sylvia. Albert and Sylvia were aware there was something amiss about their plea to leave Siam, and that they were in severe jeopardy. Sylvia's illness was under suspicion, and consequently they were in a potentially sticky financial situation, shades of the Conybeares, who had fought to go home and wound up without an income. In fact, with his letter to the Board, Albert was already doing battle for his wife and himself and their infant to get out of Siam—and to do so at the expense of the Board of Foreign Missions. He put a rosy gloss on the issue for Dr. Brown at the Foreign Missions Board. "At the Mission Meeting time, all the physicians were consulted, and they made the recommendation, which (you will see by the minutes) was unanimously approved by the Mission," he said. "Five persons voted against the certificate [Sylvia's medical certificate] itself, on the grounds that the physicians did not all agree on the details of the certificate, and hence it was thought that a new certificate should be made out."

Well, that sounded innocent, but it *really* meant that five of their fellow missionaries did not believe Sylvia was seriously ill. In the eyes of those five, Albert and Sylvia had to stay in Siam or go only in disgrace, with a mark against their name that could cause the Foreign Missions Board to take away their salary and the promised pay for their trip home, as had happened with the Conybeares.

Sylvia was only following doctors' orders, Albert insisted. He told the Foreign Missions Board that their physicians had told Sylvia to stick around in Bangkok until the end of January or early February, which would round out Siam's cool season (which was, of course, none too cool—the temperature averaged 77 degrees in the cool season ). Then, doctors advised, the Caldwells should go to southern Italy "for a few weeks, until Spring fully opens. That is what we are planning to do, unless Mrs. Caldwell's condition becomes critical, in which case the Mission has voted that we be allowed to go at once," Albert said. He hedged his argument somewhat. Yes, he admitted, some of the missionaries thought Sylvia would improve over the cool season. These were probably the five who had pooh-poohed the medical report. Those colleagues, he admitted, thought that if Sylvia improved, the Caldwells could stay in Siam and fulfill their obligations. This, however, was not an option, Albert insisted. "Our physicians have told me that it would not be safe to remain during another hot season, and that we should be running a great risk," he pleaded with the board. "That we must return to America, then, is certain."

Albert portrayed the situation as an open-and-shut case of neurasthenia, but it wasn't that simple. Apparently there was general suspicion from older and wiser missionaries who felt they understood pregnancy, childbirth, and recovery better than these frantic new parents did. But that issue was a trifle compared to the damage unintentionally inflicted several months earlier by Conybeare when he had let slip that certain missionaries were stealthily stashing away money to get out of mission work by buying their own passage home before their contracts were up. As a result, suspicion now turned on Sylvia and Albert for perhaps drumming up a medical problem when their intent had, all along, been to wiggle out of their contract—and, if you looked at it only from the money angle, it was a suspicion that had a great deal of merit. It was supposed to be a secret that they had indeed accumulated a clandestine nest egg, but Conybeare's catfight with the same people now toying with the Caldwells had revealed the hush-hush savings and had put them in the crosshairs of doubt.

It's not entirely surprising that the mission didn't congratulate them on saving money, although self-restraint in matters of money and saving for the future were surely among the Christian virtues. The church had spent a substantial sum to train the Caldwells, outfit them, and get them to Siam, and the church expected its full measure of work out of them (and had not gotten much from Sylvia in the past year). It seemed that in the church's mind, the Caldwells were pretty much committed for five years to life; that is, their furlough was due up in five years, and they had planned to stay in Siam for life. The church did not offer an easy way out of that commitment. If the Caldwells were feeling trapped, it seemed they had little choice but to flee against the church's will. And now a lot of key people thought that was exactly what they were doing, in collusion with Dr. Walker.

R. C. JONES, CHAIRMAN OF the Siam mission's Executive Committee, came up with an ominous plan. The Board of Foreign Missions should not let the matter rest, he insisted. The Board had yet to make a final ruling on the Caldwells' proposal to return to the United States, and Jones tried to jump in with an official directive as the chief missionary on the ground in Siam. He wrote to the Board in New York, "I think the best thing to do for all concerned, in case the Board gives permission [for the Caldwells] to return to America, is to have one or more of the Board's Drs. examine Mrs. Caldwell in America before settling their account." Jones said this should be done to remove all possible doubt from the Caldwells' record. Indeed, an examination might also find Sylvia well enough so that the Board could demand the church's money back for the Caldwells' return trip from Siam. Perhaps the young couple would even be intimidated enough to stay in the field. Jones knew this very well. Perhaps word of this plan reached Sylvia and Albert, but if not, they almost surely figured out that it might be coming. It was too similar to the Conybeares' battle not to invite comparison.

Not surprisingly, Dr. Walker was livid about the doubt swirling around his diagnosis. He resigned soon after, first stating as his reason that his missionary's pay was too low for him and his new wife to survive on. Someone else suggested that pay was not the real issue; rather, he was embarrassed to be the subject of gossip. Walker, while single, had "given attention" to some ladies on the mission staff, causing tongues to wag. Then he came back from furlough with a new wife, causing disappointments among the former girlfriends and further embarrassment for everyone in the tittle-tattle that inevitably followed. No, another of the mission chimed in, that wasn't why Walker was angry. It was more that he was irate about the reaction of the other missionaries to the Caldwell diagnosis.

It seemed that the diagnosis was really the most significant of those three excuses. W. G. McClure told the Board of Foreign Missions that a frustrating issue regarding Walker was

> the granting of permission to the Caldwells to return to the U.S. I suppose it is a necessity, but it is one of the greatest disappointments that we have experienced in our work. It is difficult for any of us to feel that relief [for Sylvia's health problems] could not have been had on the field [i.e., locally]. We do not blame them, but it is difficult to persuade ourselves that they had the wisest medical advice.

Later McClure reiterated in regard to Dr. Walker, "The most serious matter I think was the uncompromising position he took in the matter of the Caldwells' return to the U.S. in opposition to the opinion of the mission and of his fellow medical missionaries."

In a bitter letter to Arthur Brown of the Foreign Missions Board, Walker explained that the Bangkok missionaries "expected me, at times, to stand alongside and play second to Dr. Hansen," mainly because Hansen made no charge, so all the missionaries preferred him. Sylvia, in consulting Walker after seeing Hansen, had apparently sought a second opinion and was willing to pay for it. This fact alone may have made it look to her colleagues as though she bought a diagnosis from Walker, since they normally got their medical services for free from Hansen. Answering charges of ugliness in the Siam station, Walker said, "Yes others have had heartaches as well. If you wish to learn anything further concerning the unpleasant relations which some of us have had to bear with our missionary brethren, kindly write to Mr. and Mrs. Caldwell or to Mr. and Mrs. Conybeare or to some who are in the service yet, but would go home if they were more favorably situated financially." Walker's letter was written as his resignation went before various officials for approval, long after the Caldwells had limped home, so probably the "unpleasant relations" referred to their fight to leave. Or perhaps the Caldwells had been ill treated before Sylvia's diagnosis. Perhaps they had even been threatened with a transfer to a remote location, as the Conybeares had. In any case, Walker snarled, "Have no fear! We are not missed." The mission, he insisted, was glad to see him go.

Walker's trouble was still brewing and had not exploded in September 1911, when he told Sylvia and Albert that they must leave Siam for Sylvia's sake. Thanks to Conybeare's assertion that some had been secretly setting aside money to go home, however, the implications were that the Caldwells were staging an escape.

But the Caldwells' departure might have been more legitimate than the other missionaries thought. After all, Sylvia had not been to work all the school year. She had struggled with pregnancy and fever afterward. She and Albert were scared nearly out of their minds about the similarity of her case to that of the unfortunate Mrs. Barrett. It would scarcely do for Albert to have to raise a baby in the company of a candidate for the lunatic asylum. That thought so influenced Albert that the mission knew it would get no solid work out of him. According to R. C. Jones, "The Mission voted to have them go home only because it looked as if they would not be of further service, worth while, to the Mission." Jones fingered Walker's alarmist statement about Mrs. Barrett as causing the Caldwells to completely lose their reason in the matter.

Jones intimated that other doctors had weighed in on Sylvia's case, and the only one who agreed with Walker was Hansen, "who of course is not a missionary. It is a case full of uncertainty and we are doubtful as to what is the wise thing to do."

The Presbyterian Board of Foreign Missions accepted the Caldwells' resignations on November 6, 1911. Eight days later, the Board received Jones's suggestion that officials have Sylvia examined by Board-appointed doctors when she reached the United States, before the Board settled the Caldwells' account.

To their credit, Sylvia and Albert did everything they could to see their departure through in the right way. They followed doctors' orders and did not leave immediately, obediently remaining in Siam through the cooler

*Sylvia, Albert, and Alden Caldwell photographed in Siam. Their white clothing and Sylvia's short sleeves helped ward off the heat.*

season. They stayed on for five unhappy months after her diagnosis, no doubt running into the five who had voted against them and allowing the Board of Foreign Missions plenty of time to think about Jones' recommendation to have Sylvia examined upon reaching home.

For his part, Albert kept working and thereby won the admiration of his boss, W. G. McClure. "Mr Caldwell did full work until the date of his departure," Alice Ellinwood wrote in a letter, quoting McClure's applause for Albert. "Mr Caldwell was able to practically finish his work for the year and to examine some of his classes, and for the others he left examination questions already prepared."

DURING THE SEEMINGLY INTERMINABLE five months between the diagnosis in September and their departure in February, the Caldwells did get to see some history. The week their resignation was accepted in New York in November 1911, the Prince of Pitsanuloke, second in line to the throne of Siam, came home from a trip to England, where he had represented Siam in the coronation of England's King George V. The Prince had arrived in Bangkok in time for the upcoming coronation of the new king of Siam. As the embattled Dr. Walker described it:

> During this same week a unique and novel ceremony was witnessed by the residents of Bangkok upon the arrival of a young white elephant from the North. White elephants become the property of the King and are kept at the palace because of the good luck they bring with them. At the same time a small white monkey, caught in the jungles of the North, was also presented to His Majesty. His Majesty gave the sum of $190 [$4,625 today] as a gift to the owner of this strange little monkey. The little fellow is full of life and mischief and is now on exhibition, together with the young elephant, in a beautiful, large pavilion especially built for them.

Perhaps Albert, Sylvia, and little Alden went to see the exhibit, if Sylvia was not too ill. As they extended their stay ever longer in Siam, they saw an epoch change. In late 1911, the Oxford-educated crown prince Maha Vajiravudh was crowned Rama VI, King of Siam.

Bangkok was a sight to behold. "His Siamese Majesty and the Princes of the realm have spared neither pains nor money in preparing Bangkok for the many European Princes and Special Envoys who came as guests of His Majesty during the coronation festivities," Walker reported. "Bangkok, in many parts, was turned into fairyland. The streets were re-gravelled, rolled and prettily decorated with flags, banners and lanterns. The illuminations along the river and on the streets of the capital city were gorgeous." The revelry went on for ten days, featuring royal dinners, theatre performances, a fair, a military review, a pageant on the river, a ball hosted by the mayor, "until finally His Majesty appeared in a triumphal procession in full royal robes with all the gorgeous pomp and glory befitting a monarch of Siam," Walker described. Indeed, it was something to see, and Albert, at least, drank it in.

Sylvia probably did, too, unless she was too ill to care. She was one of the 37,169 patients treated in the ten Presbyterian hospitals and nine dispensaries in Siam and Laos in 1911. A report from the Siam/Laos mission (Laos was considered part of Siam) noted that there were 33 organized Presbyterian churches in the region with 5,519 communicants, 67 Sunday Schools with 4,282 students, and 38 Presbyterian schools with 1,487 students. That number included the children Albert and Sylvia had labored to teach. There was also a printing press that had put out an impressive four million pages in the year. There were 161 Siamese working in American Presbyterian missions in the country, and there were 88 American Presbyterian missionaries in 1911. But Albert and Sylvia were no longer numbered among them.

Although they were relieved to be released, it stung Albert to be leaving early, his hoped-for career in shambles. Albert would have stayed on if he could have. But he and Sylvia could salve the smarting pain of disappointment by enjoying the healthful balms of Italy and by accomplishing something even greater, a personal victory pulled out of the jaws of defeat. They would go home via the Atlantic, "thereby," as Albert put it, "circumnavigating the globe."

They could not know that the achievement of circumnavigation would be all but forgotten by the time they finally reached home.

# 4

## DELIVER US FROM SEASICKNESS

In late February of 1912, the Caldwells packed all their belongings, including things they had not had on the trip over: money, baby clothes, Siamese souvenirs, records of Alden's birth. They also packed gifts they had gotten for their wedding and things bought with the money the church had given them to purchase their "outfit" in 1909, which altogether included silverware, table linen, and household effects, alongside their clothing. They used a good, sturdy trunk with a stout lock, because $100 ($2,183 today) of their money was in American gold coins, which were legal tender at the time. They had bought the gold pieces with the illicit savings that Conybeare had unfortunately mentioned to mission officials. Albert had acquired the gold coins from a sailor arriving in Bangkok from America. The Caldwells' salary was paid in Siamese ticals, and they needed American money, so Albert swapped ticals for dollars with the sailor. It wasn't easy to get rid of American gold pieces in Siam, and the sailor was as glad to find Albert as vice versa. Albert tucked the gold pieces "in a little sack and put it in the bottom of my trunk" to keep them out of sight and safe. The gold pieces were a thrifty solution to a problem: they had checked into exchanging their covert savings from ticals to dollars at the bank, but the bank charged a 20 percent commission—too much, Sylvia complained.

That $100 was their seed money to start over again back in the States. It would pair up nicely with the household goods and clothing they were also bringing, making a smooth transition back into the Midwest. Because they had been approved to resign, they had (or assumed they had) the promised transportation allotment from the Presbyterians to get home, and perhaps they could count on the church or their salary to pay for the "rest cure" in Italy as prescribed by Drs. Walker and Hansen. Rest was a common cure for neurasthenia. Given the brouhaha over their leaving, however, Albert and Sylvia may have been worried that their financial standing with the church was in doubt. Perhaps they were already nervous that the church might demand its money back for any salary they were still getting, the rest cure, their travel, their "outfit," or all of those things.

Sylvia packed up Alden's few belongings for the trip, no doubt worrying at least a little about how difficult it would be to travel with an infant. The trip would be even harder than normal, because it appears clear today that Sylvia couldn't hold the baby. Apparently she was able to rest him in her lap, but actively holding him in her arms was a problem. This was perhaps a result of neurasthenia, as many patients reported numbness in arms or legs. She had been unwell and not working for many months and perhaps had been in bed a lot, so maybe she was just too weak to hold a heavy, wriggling baby. Regardless, the fact that she couldn't hold Alden shortly became critical to Albert's survival on the *Titanic*.

THEY HAD NOT YET even heard of the *Titanic*, though, and Albert was up to the challenge of tending Alden. He could tote the baby around on their journey home. They left Siam on February 21 or 22, 1912. They took "a little, poky steamer," as Albert described it, down to Singapore, some eight hundred miles away. "Little" and "poky" probably added up to seasickness for poor Sylvia, so she was no doubt relieved in Singapore when they boarded a larger, faster German liner—probably the *Derfflinger*—bound for Europe via the Indian Ocean. The ship, of the Lloyd line, took them through an assortment of exotic ports: the British colony of Penang; Colombo, strategically located for trade on the coast of Ceylon; Aden, at the bottom edge of mysterious Arabia; Suez in Egypt via the Biblical Red Sea; and through the Suez Canal. Soon, Sylvia was seasick again. They left Port Said in Egypt and continued onward, with Sylvia struggling with seasickness much of the way. The Lloyd liner went on to England, but the Caldwells got off in Naples, Italy, just as they had planned, a grueling month after they had left Bangkok. The rest cure probably sounded pretty good to them.

But there was dreadful news in Naples. A cholera epidemic had swept through the city the year before. It had been kept a secret from the world at large, but word was leaching out. On March 8 and 9, about a week before the Caldwells arrived in Naples, the Italian parliament had discussed the epidemic in regards to funding for public health agencies. One government official counterintuitively went on the record to state the policy of keeping the epidemic quiet. He felt that the disease would be overblown in the foreign media. Thus, although cholera news was officially suppressed, the censored information was at last getting out. The Italian government had begun inspecting hygienic conditions in Naples and was appalled; perhaps word of this was flying around Naples as well.

The Caldwells had planned to enjoy Naples and southern Italy, as they had promised the doctors in Siam. But then they apparently heard about the cholera epidemic. Sylvia was so weak, and Alden was so small. It seemed folly to rest in a cholera-prone city; the "rest" they got might be of the eternal variety. So Sylvia and Albert changed their minds about relaxing in southern Italy. They quickly had to figure out what to do next.

One possibility was immediate passage to America. It wasn't the ideal plan; they had meant for Sylvia to take her prescribed break. However, they toyed with the idea as they looked over Naples' harbor. "I saw a boat with the American flag at the foremast, which was a signal that she was leaving for America that day," Albert recalled. He turned to a sailor and asked, "What boat is that?" The sailor replied, "That's a Cunard boat, the *Carpathia*, which is leaving for New York today." They considered taking the *Carpathia* and perhaps even sought tickets. But if so, Sylvia nixed the idea. She had most likely been queasy on the dinky boat from Siam and had certainly been green around the gills on the Lloyd liner through the Mediterranean. The *Carpathia* looked about the same size as the *Derfflinger*, and that size meant a lot of rolling on the ocean. Sylvia wanted to go home on a larger boat boat, one that would be more stable and less likely to twist her stomach into nausea.

The search didn't take long. They checked into a hotel, and there they saw a placard advertising a new ship, the *Titanic*, as "a new triple screw steamer of the White Star Line," taking its maiden voyage from England on April 10. It was almost exactly the date they had planned to leave for home. And best of all it was huge—the largest liner in the world. If any ship could deliver Sylvia from seasickness, that was the one. Albert turned to Sylvia and said, "Well, that's the boat we're going to take across the Atlantic." Sylvia was thrilled.

That put an end to an Italian rest cure, but all sorts of lovely possibilities sprang to mind. Certainly Sylvia could restore some of her strength with solid earth under her feet and some good European cooking to revive her body and spirit. The Caldwells would take the land route through Europe, letting Sylvia rest as much as she could as they saw sights and enjoyed the cooler weather. They would be home soon enough, anyway, and then she could *really* rest. To catch the huge new ocean liner, they had to get to England, so they plotted a way northward through cities they wanted to see, probably going from city to city by train, a means and itinerary then touted as a cheap, friendly trip for people of small or moderate means.

Thus, Albert, Sylvia, and baby Alden spent several interesting weeks touring Europe on their way to England. They had certainly come up in the world. A few short years ago they were too poor to pay for an education, and a few short months ago they were missionaries working in the sweltering tropics. Now they were tourists, gawking at the sights of Europe. They went from Naples to Florence, home to the famous Duomo and the even more famous David. From there they went up to Venice, where they admired the gondolas gliding through the canals. They dipped into enchanting Lucerne, Switzerland, with its unmatched scenery and stunning lake, and then went over to cosmopolitan Paris. There they bought new clothes. The Caldwells were going home in style.

The European trail ended in London, where they stayed at 2 Upper Montague Street. London was cold, and that compelled them to do more shopping—for wool clothing. After living in the tropics, their wardrobes were sadly lacking for cold weather. They would need warmer clothing in a climate that actually had winters.

BUT THE MORE IMPORTANT purchase was passage home on that ship they had seen advertised, the *Titanic*. "Upon reaching London I went to the White Star Office to get reservations on the *Titanic*," Albert said. The news wasn't good. The clerk said the second class tickets were all sold out. It turned out the ship was a tourism magnet. The clerk told Albert that many people had come over from Canada and America just to go back on this new, beautiful White Star liner on its maiden voyage. Albert was in anguish—he had not expected this.

He was outgoing. He was friendly. He "kind of got on the good side of the clerks there," as he admitted later. After some chat, he asked, "Isn't there *any* possibility of getting a reservation on the *Titanic*?" He looked pretty crestfallen about the situation; it was clear to the clerk that this young fellow really wanted a ticket. The clerk said, "I tell you what. Every day there's a cancellation. Come back tomorrow, and maybe we'll have one. If you wait around all day, you can have the first cancellation that comes in."

It was an agonizing wait the next day. Albert and Sylvia had enough money from their church allotment to cover passage in second class—£29 ($2,919 today) —but they really shouldn't break into those gold pieces reserved for starting over in the Midwest. Nevertheless, Albert resolved that he'd take a first class ticket if that's what got cancelled. He'd even take a third class ticket, although he and Sylvia were middle class now and would not fit in with the immigrants in third class. But they *really* wanted to take the *Titanic*. Sylvia *really* needed that big, stable boat. She couldn't recuperate from neurasthenia if she were constantly battling nausea.

Finally a cancellation came in. It was second class—just what they had hoped for! The Caldwells would be going home on the *Titanic*.

They eagerly let various relatives know that they'd arrive in New York on April 17 on the exciting new *Titanic*, and they told the Foreign Missions Board they would be going home to the senior Caldwells' residence in Illinois after that. One person they notified was Albert's cousin, Dr. Charles Swan Caldwell, who lived near Pittsburgh, as they planned to go through Pittsburgh on the way home. Perhaps they planned for Sylvia to see him professionally about her illness. Sylvia must have already been improving, though, because they seemed to have had a good time in Europe. The trip perhaps made up for the hasty excuse for a honeymoon on their way to mission work two and a half years ago. Now Albert and Sylvia were enjoying Europe on a tour that in previous centuries only the wealthy could aspire to. Yes, indeed, they really *had* come up in the world.

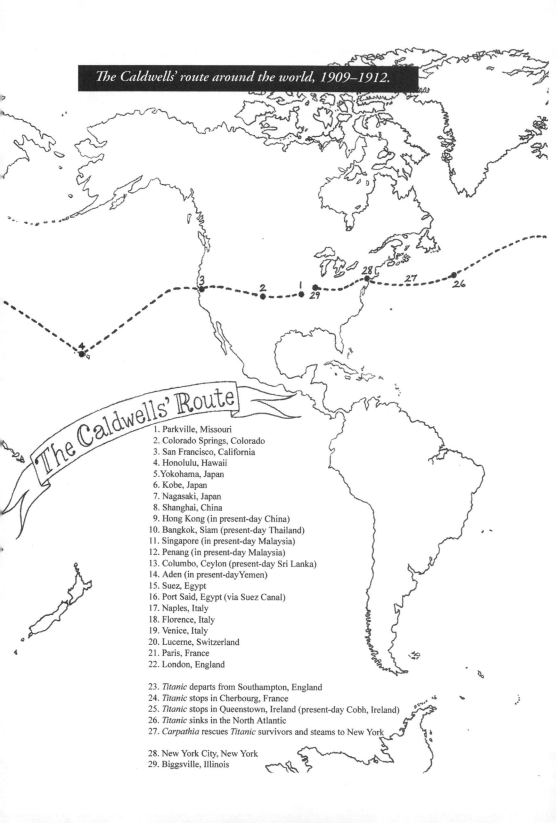

The Caldwells' route around the world, 1909–1912.

**The Caldwells' Route**

1. Parkville, Missouri
2. Colorado Springs, Colorado
3. San Francisco, California
4. Honolulu, Hawaii
5. Yokohama, Japan
6. Kobe, Japan
7. Nagasaki, Japan
8. Shanghai, China
9. Hong Kong (in present-day China)
10. Bangkok, Siam (present-day Thailand)
11. Singapore (in present-day Malaysia)
12. Penang (in present-day Malaysia)
13. Columbo, Ceylon (present-day Sri Lanka)
14. Aden (in present-day Yemen)
15. Suez, Egypt
16. Port Said, Egypt (via Suez Canal)
17. Naples, Italy
18. Florence, Italy
19. Venice, Italy
20. Lucerne, Switzerland
21. Paris, France
22. London, England

23. *Titanic* departs from Southampton, England
24. *Titanic* stops in Cherbourg, France
25. *Titanic* stops in Queenstown, Ireland (present-day Cobh, Ireland)
26. *Titanic* sinks in the North Atlantic
27. *Carpathia* rescues *Titanic* survivors and steams to New York

28. New York City, New York
29. Biggsville, Illinois

Jan Hedgepeth Wright 2010

On April 10, 1912, the day Alden turned 10 months old, their European trip nominally came to an end—and yet it seemed their vacation would go on as it unfolded into a luxurious journey home, a sparkling conclusion to their sometimes depressing and recently oppressive careers overseas. They climbed onto the steamer train from Waterloo Station bound to Southampton, the port of London. The train click-click-clicked along the rails to the *Titanic*. What a privilege to be traveling on the finest liner ever built!—at least, that's how Albert described it, starry-eyed. The only ship that could match the *Titanic* was her sister, *Olympic*. As Albert told it, people "congratulated themselves on sharing with others the maiden trip of the most wonderful boat ever launched."

The *Titanic* was well hyped. By now the Caldwells had heard all the soaring adjectives and mighty claims. Most marvelous, in Albert's mind, was the fact that the *Titanic* was unsinkable. They had apparently heard a sales pitch: "Watertight compartments which could be closed would render the boat absolutely secure and non-sinkable—so we were told," Albert recalled later. As one admiring reporter of the day put it:

> Safety is the first consideration with all voyagers and no excellence can compensate for the lack of it. *Titanic* is the last word in this respect, double bottom and watertight compartments, steel decks, massive steel plates all in their way making for security, safety and strength. Nothing is left to chance: every mechanical device that could be conceived has been employed to further secure immunity from risk either by sinking or by fire. Should disaster overtake her through contact with rock, instant means can be taken to avert the consequences . . . [The officer in charge] is enabled at the same time by the moving of a lever to close up and seal all or any watertight compartments into which the ship is divided. The dangers of the sea, therefore, are practically non-existent on this latest magnificent vessel.

Sylvia was skeptical that the ship was really unsinkable. Not that her skepticism dimmed the excitement. A friend accompanied them from London with a camera, ready to photograph such a remarkable ship. Everyone wanted to see the fine ocean liner, and their friend was surely pleased to have an excuse to get on board as he saw them off.

At dockside they watched the porters moving luggage, including their own. Albert probably would not have handled their luggage anyway—they were moving up in the world, after all, and would have used a porter—but in this case it was imperative. He had to carry Alden, as Sylvia was still ailing and could not. Sylvia did, however, turn to a porter, anxious to satisfy that nagging question about that claim she didn't quite believe. "Is this ship really nonsinkable?" she asked. He replied, "Yes, lady. God himself could not sink this ship."

As their travel trunk made its way to their cabin near the stern in the capable hands of a porter, they boarded via the second class gangway and looked around as best they could, drinking in the wonders of the largest ship in the world. The weather was overcast and chilly. Little Alden was swaddled in multiple layers and a little hat. Albert had on a jaunty cap topping off a smart suit and tie, and Sylvia wore a sweater over her skirt and blouse, a nautical hat atop her head. Gray though it was, it was a good opportunity for a picture. Their friend suggested they pose against the railing outside the second class smoking room, next to a gate that led down to another deck. The sky above was blotted with dreary clouds, and behind them loomed the striped smokestacks of two ships dwarfed by the *Titanic*, the *St. Louis* and the *Philadelphia* of the American line. A huge cable came down behind the Caldwells, and a ladder scrambled upward to the right of Sylvia. Just over their shoulders in the background hung a couple of lifeboats on the *St. Louis*. The *St. Louis* might need such things, but the *Titanic's* own lifeboats were pretty much useless, according to the enthusiastic publicity. Sylvia leaned over to be sure Alden, in his daddy's arms, was happy. Due to her ongoing weakness, she propped her elbow on the railing of the *Titanic* for support. Just at that moment as Sylvia looked away, their friend snapped the photo. Their friend promised to send the photo to them in America when it was developed.

The *Titanic* was truly beautiful. Albert and Sylvia couldn't help but draw comparisons to the poky little steamer leaving Siam so recently or to the pitching and rolling *Manchuria* that had taught them about seasickness

*The Caldwells on the* Titanic *on sailing day, April 10, 1912. Behind them are the lifeboats on the* St. Louis. *A friend allowed on board briefly before the sailing took the photo and sent it to them later. The original of the photo is only three by four inches, so it has been enlarged here and on the cover of this book.*

across the Pacific in 1909. This was so much better, so much more opulent, and *SO* huge. "She was equipped with all the conveniences that one would desire," Albert recalled. It was certainly more luxurious than anything they had ever traveled in. There were squash courts and Turkish baths, a swimming pool, multiple dining rooms. Even the corridors were beautiful. There were electric elevators between decks, a novelty that *everyone* was amazed to see. To Albert, they seemed a marvel of modern technology. The ship was the finest transportation that travel money could buy. For the couple who had spent their entire married life in Siam, it seemed as though they had landed in a floating English fairy tale.

The ship was also amazingly fast; as soon as she got out to sea, the *Titanic* seemed to be traveling at record speed across the ocean, and the crew posted the day's speed and distance covered as a public relations ploy. It was like flying. The *Manchuria* had plodded across the Pacific in six weeks, and the poky steamer and German liner had taken a month to get them from Bangkok to Naples. The fast track across the Atlantic was therefore quite amazing. Albert and everyone else were "watching, with interest, the record speed that we were making." No one worried about such speed being hazardous. "Danger was the last thought in our minds," Albert said.

The bunkbeds in their small cabin might have been the only thing that reminded them they weren't traveling first class, where passengers got luxurious double beds. Albert took the top bunk and Sylvia shared the bottom bunk with the baby. The room had a dresser and its own sink; a shared bathroom was down the hall. There was a spot for their travel trunk in their room, its locked lid concealing the American gold pieces. Thanks to the trunk they didn't need to entrust the gold to the purser, as other passengers did with their money.

Albert recalled, "The sea was calm, the weather was nice, everybody was having a good time." Best of all, "No one was sea sick." Sylvia was absolutely loving it—she was *not* seasick. It was a good thing, too, because the dining tables in second class were "piled with all the luxuries and delicacies" anyone could ever want, as Albert described. The Caldwells ate well, and Sylvia was delighted that she could enjoy the food without nausea. For breakfast on April 11, they could choose from fruit, rolled oats, boiled hominy, fresh fish, Yarmouth bloaters (which meant grilled herring ), grilled ox, kidneys and bacon, American dry hash au gratin, grilled sausage, mashed potatoes, grilled ham and fried eggs, fried potatoes, Vienna and Graham rolls, soda scones, buckwheat cakes, maple syrup, conserve, marmalade—Albert loved marmalade—watercress, tea, and coffee. For dinner on the night of April 14, the Caldwells and fellow second class travelers selected from consommé, tapioca, baked haddock with sharp sauce, curried chicken and rice, spring lamb with mint sauce, roast turkey with cranberry sauce, green peas, pureed turnips, boiled rice, boiled and roasted potatoes, plum pudding, wine jelly, a dessert called a "cocoanut sandwich," American ice cream, assorted nuts, fresh fruit, cheese, biscuits (which meant cookies), and coffee. There were other amenities, too—stewardesses would fetch you a glass of milk if you wanted, and you could enjoy the *Titanic* band, which performed all over the ship, including outside the library where second class travelers could find a book to read. Albert and Sylvia never lacked for entertainment. Music was not merely a first class privilege. They could hear music almost whenever they wished to.

Indeed, this was the rest cure in style.

Just as delightful was the camaraderie in the second class dining room. Alden was cute and attracted attention. The Caldwells sat at dinner with Harvey and Lottie Collyer and their little girl, Marjorie, who went by "Madge" and who no doubt liked Alden. The Collyers were emigrating from England to Idaho, where Harvey intended to start a fruit farm. The Collyers, too, were thrilled with the food and with the ship in general. Harvey scrawled a quick letter to his parents, which he posted when the *Titanic* stopped at Queenstown, Ireland. "Well dears," he wrote, "so far we are having a delightful trip the weather is beautiful and the ship magnificent. We can't describe the tables it's like a floating town . . . There is hardly any motion she is so large we have not felt sick yet . . ." Perhaps the Caldwells also met Hilda Slayter in the dining room. She was one of the Canadians Albert had been told were taking the voyage, although she had not come over specifically to take the *Titanic*.

Best of all there was that enormous ship, which offered many curiosities to investigate. "I enjoyed going all down inside the boat, exploring it—this great vessel," Albert later recalled. And there was so *much* to explore. "She was over three city blocks long," he added a little wistfully later, remembering how much fun she had been to discover. *Titanic* weighed around 53,000 tons and was more than 882 feet long. She was as tall as a ten-story skyscraper, and that didn't count her towering funnels. Those electric elevators up and down the ten decks were not only little pieces of genius, but they were also quite handy for poking around such a huge ocean liner. Albert took his camera and tripod with him all over the *Titanic*.

Other passengers might be enjoying amenities such as the gymnasium or the swimming pool, but he wanted to see where the *real* action was. While Sylvia stayed in the cabin with Alden one day, recuperating and letting Alden nap, Albert headed out to see the engine room. He convinced someone—one of the crewmen—to give him a behind-the-scenes tour. It wasn't too hard—Albert was a glib talker.

He and the crewman made their way down, down, past the areas where passengers normally visited, and into the realm of crew only. Albert was privileged to be there, which he relished. What things to see! The engines—remarkable!—he saw two big engines and one small one, probably a steam turbine. The machinery was enormous, so immense that the hulks extended well above the catwalk high overhead, out of Albert's range of vision. He stared up in awe. This was the ship's heartbeat. All of this marvelous equipment powered the propellers to produce that record speed that everyone was noting so admiringly so many decks above.

That wasn't all; no, there were also the furnaces on the *gigantic* boilers, another thrilling wonder of technology. Albert was fascinated with the sweaty, grimy stokers, busy feeding the boilers by tossing coal into the fires with their shovels. He asked if he could take their picture and, in fact, if he could make the ship go, too, by tossing coal into the fire. The stokers were amused by his interest and even more amused when this schoolteacher wanted a photo of himself shoveling coal. Albert introduced himself and set his camera up on its tripod before he posed with a stoker's shovel, perhaps that of Frederick Barrett. Someone snapped the picture as the stokers egged him on. They loved this attention. To Albert, it was fun—dirty, hot, and *really* fun.

This was a rare moment on the segregated *Titanic*. Normally a passenger would contact the crew only insofar as the crew served the passenger. Passengers converse with stokers and shovel coal? Not normally. But that was Albert. He had worked with people in Siam who would have been thought downtrodden and ignorant by the average American. Albert liked those people, and he liked these stokers, too. He made an impression on the stokers, an impression that ultimately saved his life.

Albert got lots more pictures all over the ship, for a future photo album that little Alden would someday enjoy, a souvenir of their fairy tale trip. Too bad Alden was so small he wouldn't remember it. The pictures would help. Albert was sure they'd all love looking back on and reliving this wonderful voyage.

# 5

# To the Lifeboats—
# Women and Children First!

Even the weather was pleasant enough, considering it was the North Atlantic in April. On Sunday the 14th, however, the temperature began falling, and by afternoon it was so nippy the Caldwells decided to stay in their cabin rather than stroll the deck with the baby. Unfortunately, Alden put up a squall. Perhaps he was angry about being cooped up. Or maybe—being acclimated to Siam, where the average daily temperature never got below 69 degrees and the average daily high was in the 90s —he was fussing about being cold. Or perhaps he was just having a bad baby day.

Whatever the reason, Alden's crying was disturbing the Sunday peace. Surely the neighboring cabins could hear him. There weren't enough playthings to distract Alden. In desperation, Sylvia or Albert turned their keys into a baby's rattle, shaking them before the wailing child. It worked. Thank goodness, Alden liked the keys. In fact, he insisted on having the keys and wouldn't let them go. That was okay. It was keeping him quiet. Alden happily shook and fingered the keys. When he lost them, his parents didn't realize it. There was no reason for them even to think of the keys again.

By that evening, the temperature had dropped to bone-chillingly cold. The Caldwells attended a church service in the second class dining room that Sunday night, but they had not stopped to get Alden's warm things out of the trunk—they held the baby tight to keep him warm as they realized how sharply the temperature had plummeted.

The service was popular. An English clergyman led the event, which was packed with worshippers—happy worshippers, Albert thought. They were all happy to be worshipping God. They prayed. The Reverend Mr. Carter "took as his subject 'The Perils of the Sea,' comparing the perils of

life to the perils of the sea," Albert recalled. It was an abstract homily, rife
with symbolism that the ocean travelers, safe and secure that night, only
imagined that they understood. They understood the lesson to refer to the
general perils of life, the ups and downs faced by the soul as it was tossed to
and fro on the waves of life. It did not mean *literal* danger. They were on an
unsinkable ship, after all, so they in no way were suffering from the perils of
the sea. That was someone else's problem. They took it as a purely spiritual
lesson that cleverly made use of their voyage as a backdrop. No doubt the
clergyman took it that way, too. The service closed with the congregation
singing the 1860 classic hymn, "For Those in Peril on the Sea":

> Eternal Father, strong to save
> Whose arm hath bound the restless wave.
> Who bidd'st the mighty ocean deep
> Its own appointed limits keep
> Oh hear us when we cry to thee
> For those in peril on the sea.
>
> O Trinity of love and power
> Our brethren shield in danger's hour
> From rock and tempest, fire and foe
> Protect them wheresoe'er they go.
> Thus evermore shall rise to Thee
> Glad hymns of praise from land and sea.

Albert took a walk around the deck before bed, a pleasant if arctic
way to unwind. It was the kind of night that would make anyone want
to snuggle under a warm blanket. They went to bed about 10 o'clock. As
Sylvia said, "The night was *cold* [she underlined "cold"] so we went to bed
to keep warm." Albert climbed into his top bunk, and Sylvia and Alden
crawled into the lower bunk. Albert liked the upper bunk. Situated mid-air
as it was, it vibrated soothingly in the rhythm of the engines. Soon he was
peacefully asleep.

For Sylvia, with the baby in her bed, it was not quite so peaceful. Anyone sharing a bed with a baby is by definition a light sleeper. As Alden wiggled and called out and fretted in his sleep, she hurriedly soothed him back to quietness. The baby was restless, and as a result, she was dozing lightly at 11:40, when she felt a sudden shudder of the ship. It felt to her "as if a large dog had a baby kitten in its mouth and was shaking it."

"Albert," she called softly, trying to wake him up without waking Alden.

**ALBERT WOKE WITHOUT REALIZING** Sylvia had been calling him. He would later say he was awakened by the sheer stillness of the ship. The bed no longer hummed with its soothing vibrations. It was like riding a Pullman sleeper train, he thought. The click-click-click of the rails blended into a mass of pleasing noise that shut out the world. But you woke up when that rhythm stopped. This was the same.

He knew instantly that the engines had stopped, but unlike passengers in that Pullman sleeper, the passengers on the *Titanic* were not at their destination yet. "What in the world are the engines stopped this time of night for?" he wondered. He got up and threw his raincoat over his pajamas and went out onto the deck. He spotted a sailor looking over into the water. "What's wrong?" he asked.

"Oh," the sailor said casually, "we've just bumped into an iceberg. It didn't do any harm, I guess."

"I should think we had, from the chill of the atmosphere," Albert replied.

Albert went back into the cabin and told Sylvia about the iceberg in a quiet voice—so as not to awaken Alden—and crawled back up to the top bunk to go back to sleep. Not that it was easy to get back to sleep. He hadn't realized how much he had counted on the soothing vibration of the upper bunk. Confound the engines being off, when he himself had made them go! He hoped the stokers would be tossing coal into the fires again quickly.

Albert drifted off to sleep again for the last few moments of peace he would know for many days. Sylvia, however, could not go back to sleep. "I was nervous and wakeful and could not sleep, and it was well that this was true," she recalled later, because she heard a gong ringing and a seaman running by and shouting, "Everyone on deck with his lifebelt!" He was running too fast. If Sylvia hadn't been awake, "I would never have heard him," she said. Luckily, another crewman followed the first, pounding on the cabin door. "Everybody on deck!" he yelled. "Everybody on deck with your lifebelt!"

Albert awakened again. He was cross. How foolish it was, he thought, for them to get up everyone, his baby included, at this hour of the night. Alden had been so fussy earlier, and that's exactly what *nobody* needed— a howling baby who would be tuning up just when the excitement had passed and everyone would be going back to bed. It was a young parent's nightmare. Really, what *was* the crew thinking? Why didn't they at least wait until morning? The boat couldn't sink, anyhow, so what was the rush about?

Calling forth the patience of a missionary exercising compassion for the misguided, Albert decided that the crew was following the rules of the sea in rousing the passengers after the collision. Sylvia and Alden were now up anyway. Albert had been outside already; he knew how cold it was. They had to dress warmly. He changed from his pajamas into an old suit he had hanging on a hook—probably the one he had been wearing earlier that day. The old one that he picked was no doubt a little rumpled, and it certainly couldn't match the smart Parisian fashions in the trunk, awaiting their Midwestern debut. Sylvia wore her oldest clothes, too.

When they got to dressing Alden, they realized that the trunk was still locked—and *now* they discovered that the keys were gone. The baby had some warm things, including a little hat and a little coat. Those things had been locked in the trunk, and there they remained. Here it was as cold as an iceberg outside, and they couldn't get to Alden's cold-weather wardrobe. They searched fruitlessly for the missing keys, growing more and more frustrated by the minute. Where *had* Alden flung them? Sylvia was also anxious about the $100 in gold that they couldn't get to in the trunk. It was all they had, their seed money for starting over. They had worked so hard to save it on the sly. They should take it with them. But the trunk stayed locked, frustratingly locked.

Albert didn't believe there was any danger to the ship, so there was no real reason to take the cash with them. Sylvia's anxiety about the money was perhaps unsettling, as though she thought the sailors were doing more than just following the rules of the sea in bidding them to get out on deck.

Perhaps she really thought the ship might be in danger. She had felt the ship hit the iceberg, after all. Then again, perhaps she was just afraid that someone would take advantage of passengers being outside of their cabins and go through people's things. She was, in fact, worried that her jewelry might disappear as well. The one bright spot, as they struggled to find the keys to the trunk, was that there was no way any looter could open that trunk, unless he or she miraculously spotted the missing keys. And no one was finding any keys. It would have to wait until morning.

Without keys and without gold and, most importantly for the moment, without Alden's coat, the Caldwells picked up a steamer rug (more like a blanket than a rug) and wrapped a nightie-clad Alden in it. They may well have put the soft little booties that he had been wearing that day back on his feet, as it was awfully cold. Sylvia and Albert put their life jackets on—Alden was too little to fit into a life jacket—and made their way to the ice-cold top deck. "There was a great throng gathered," as Albert described it. "[It] looked like a crowd on a busy street." No one was panicking or even acting very worried. Well, there was a *little* worry, which the Caldwells detected as they overheard snatches of conversations. Someone pointed out a light at sea in the distance and said, "There's a boat over there," and someone else said, "To the worst she'll come and rescue us." Based on the lights that they could see, Albert and Sylvia guessed it was a German boat, not unlike the one they had taken across the Indian Ocean.

The German boat was comforting on the horizon, as there was surely no danger whatsoever now. At least, Albert lulled himself into thinking that, and Sylvia did, too. Crewmen told passengers over and over again that the situation was not dangerous at all, and that the *Titanic*'s sister ship, the *Olympic*, was on the way to transfer passengers and crew from the damaged (but not dangerous) *Titanic*. In fact, Sylvia was so convinced of their eminent rescue, if needed, that she comforted a nervous woman on deck. "One woman was greatly distressed and I told her that we could be transferred to the boat which could clearly be seen," Sylvia said. There was even time for small talk. Sylvia conversed with "two dear old gentlemen who were making their first trip across the Atlantic to visit their married daughter living in Rhode Island."

Albert held Alden tightly against the cold night air and worried about keeping him warm in his blanket. That was Albert's chief concern at present. Indeed, it was clear there was no need to evacuate the *Titanic* at all. It was just a waiting game until they could go back to their warm cabin. Sylvia agreed with him.

All of a sudden a crewman sang out, "To the lifeboats! Women and children first!"

"WE WERE ASTOUNDED," ALBERT recalled later. He was not in the least surprised, however, when the crew had trouble finding women and children willing to get into those insubstantial open lifeboats. The *Titanic* was clearly not in any real trouble; he was sure of that. From Albert's Midwestern point of view, it was a risky thing for women to take to small boats in mid-ocean when most had no strength for nor experience in rowing, and some would be required to tend children rather than tend oars. It seemed like a quick trip to disaster. "They [the women and children] didn't want to run this chance," Albert explained.

And how well he and Sylvia recalled her seasickness! Surely such seasickness would be exacerbated in an open boat. Albert looked over the side of the *Titanic* into the blackness, keeping Alden in his arms, well away from the steep side of the ship. The baby would be in constant danger in a small, open boat, especially if his seasick mother, still hobbled in some fashion due to neurasthenia, had to hold him. The sailors were calling for women and children, but the simple fact was that Sylvia wouldn't be able to hold the baby with confidence or ease.

The thought of sending them off the ship and into the dreadful arms of the Atlantic just wasn't palatable. "I didn't want to trust the lives of my wife and baby to one of those lifeboats into the ocean," Albert said. "I did not want to . . . see them lowered in the darkness." No one else seemed willing to do that, either. That's why, Albert noticed, the first boats rowed away "only half full of women and children who were practically forced into them."

Still, no one was overly concerned. A good people-watcher, Sylvia assessed the situation with sharp eyes. She recalled later, "There was no screaming, hysteria or violent sobbing. Here and there were little groups chatting, little knowing that at that moment the great vessel was gradually sinking."

It was so painfully cold and just as painfully obvious that they'd be standing about for some time that Sylvia sent Albert back to their cabin for another steamer rug for Alden. Albert and the baby set off through the passageways, now deserted, and found another blanket in their cabin. Perhaps Albert had one last fruitless look for the keys. As he made his way back to where he had left Sylvia, he stepped through what he thought was a watertight door, a piece of ship technology that he probably recognized (or thought he did) from his tour earlier in the voyage. He marveled that it had not been closed—which was an odd thing, if they were afraid of the ship sinking. Yet he also had to thank God that the captain had not closed the door while he was in the cabin with the baby. The open door no doubt increased his conviction *not* to put Sylvia and Alden on a lifeboat. The watertight doors hadn't been shut yet, so small was the danger. The doors still could be closed if things got bad, and everyone knew the watertight doors would keep the *Titanic* afloat indefinitely.

After Albert got back, the Caldwells followed the crew's directions to an enclosed gangway on C-Deck, where it was, thankfully, warmer. Other people accompanied them, milling about as they waited for . . . they weren't sure what, exactly. A seaman had told them they would fill the boats from that deck, but that now seemed inaccurate. It was obvious the whole operation was willy-nilly and unrehearsed. Albert and Sylvia may have recognized some people they were waiting with. One was Canadian Hilda Slayter, who had been taking music lessons in Italy and then shopping in Ireland for her wedding gown and trousseau. If Albert and Sylvia had not met her before, they perhaps chatted as they waited, and Hilda may have discerned that Albert was carrying the baby because Sylvia had trouble doing so. There was also Fanny Kelly, Hilda's cabinmate.

THEN THINGS REALLY GOT confusing, confounding the retelling of it for the next century—indeed, what follows is an educated guess that best fits an assortment of circumstances that various people described.

It appears that the Caldwells and the others finally gave up waiting and wandered back out onto the open part of C Deck, coincidentally arriving at a set of steep, utilitarian stairs identical to and a few dozen feet away from the ones the Caldwells had been photographed beside on sailing day. Of course, the Caldwells had been at the top of the stairs in second class space in the photo; now they found themselves at the bottom, in the third class area. It was perhaps no surprise that at the top now, they found that bedroom stewards had cordoned off the gate, a gate just like the one that Sylvia had been leaning near on the sailing day picture. The stewards said they were enforcing the rule of women and children first but perhaps were actually restricting male refugees from a second class deck, thinking they were steerage passengers (and the Caldwells, dressed in their oldest clothes, perhaps even looked like immigrants). Hilda Slayter recalled that at the top of the stairs, a crewman attempted to stop Albert and in fact reached to take little Alden out of his arms. According to Hilda's account written privately many years later, the crewman said, "'No men' and went to take the baby from him—I went over quickly and climbed up saying—There are no more women behind me—Mayn't he go along? and the officer let him pass." Although other accounts indicated stewards as the guards, Hilda recalled an officer letting Albert pass. Perhaps there were both. Stewards may have guarded the gate, but maybe a nearby officer agreed with Hilda's plea to let Albert past the steward battalion. If so, the officer was probably Sixth Officer James Moody, who was likely in the vicinity.

Then the Caldwells and everyone else found that someone had locked a door leading to the deck where lifeboats were actually being loaded. They searched for a way up and spotted a crew ladder attached to the wall and leading up to the deck where the boats were. Fanny Kelly, however, was not spry. She had an extremely hard time climbing up; she "was not at all active," as second class passenger Lawrence Beesley described. Hilda and Albert helped push her up the ladder.

However, it seems that Albert and his family did not go up the ladder with the others. It appears that Sylvia *couldn't* climb the ladder affixed to the wall—her illness had come into play, indicating perhaps an arm, leg, hand, or foot that did not work. It seems that this handicap was visible to the casual observer and was the same one that kept her from holding her baby, as shortly others would notice on the lifeboat.

The Caldwells waited alone, conflicted as to what to do. Then someone spotted them. "I finally heard an officer say, 'My God! There is a woman down there,'" Sylvia recounted later. The officer, perhaps Moody, lowered a rope ladder or maybe a swing-like rope device. If it was a ladder, Sylvia may have sat on the bottom rung of the ladder and been pulled up. Albert climbed up one of the ladders with the baby, a delicate, one-armed balancing act.

Freed to go to the lifeboats at last, Sylvia and Albert still were not sold on the idea of Sylvia and Alden getting into one of them. The fairy tale cruise aboard the *Titanic* had collapsed into a colossal headache, truly, but they still saw no real reason for their infant son and his vulnerable mother to leave the unsinkable ship.

# 6

## 'To See How the Sea Flap-Dragoned It'

Back in Illinois, William and Fannie Caldwell were worrying about their son and daughter-in-law and the grandchild they had never met. They knew, no doubt, that Sylvia was struggling with her health and that she suffered from seasickness. That evening, as they were getting ready for bed, William and Fannie got down on their knees for their regular evening devotions and prayed for the safe return of their son and his family. Albert was not wearing his missionary hat on the night of the sinking, and so, he always thought, it was his parents' prayers that caused what happened next.

As Sylvia and Albert were wavering over whether to put Sylvia and Alden into a lifeboat, a cluster of stokers appeared at the deck where the Caldwells now were. Sweaty, covered in black grime, some of them wet with seawater, the men looked like they had been toiling in hell. But for the Caldwells, one of these men was surely their guardian angel, sent, as Albert saw it later, by his parents' anxious prayers.

Albert was surprised when one of the stokers, perhaps Frederick Barrett, George Beauchamp, James Crimmins, or William Major, looked firmly at him and addressed him by name. "Mr. Caldwell!" It was one of the stokers he had met the day he had taken the photographs at the great ship's furnaces. The stoker approached, clearly giving Albert an order. "If you value your life, get off this ship," he said. "I've been below, and this ship is going to sink. The ocean is pouring in much faster than the pump can keep up." The other stokers seconded him by adding, "This boat's gonna sink. There's the water rushing in the hold below."

These were startling warnings. The deck was still solid beneath their feet. The *Titanic* was still unsinkable. The watertight doors were still open in nonchalant tribute to the lack of danger—at least, Albert thought they were. But there was the unmistakable and worrisome truth that women and children were indeed off in the lifeboats. And crewmen who ought to know the truth were insisting that they get off. Albert had been below where these stokers worked, and he could picture the hold that they said was now filling with water.

One deck above, Lawrence Beesley was looking down to the Caldwells' deck. Like the Reverend Caldwell back in Illinois, Beesley was praying. He had been awake when the ship hit the iceberg. Although it didn't feel like a heavy collision, the circumstances that followed had frightened him enough that he hurried to his cabin and got out his Bible, reading the 91st Psalm over and over until he calmed down. He was much comforted by its soothing message about guardian angels: "For He shall give his angels charge over thee, to keep thee in all thy ways." A former agnostic who had become a Christian Scientist, he turned next to the denomination's textbook, *Science and Health with Key to the Scriptures,* and its poetic interpretation of the 23rd Psalm: "DIVINE LOVE is my shepherd; I shall not want . . . LOVE leadeth me beside the still waters . . ." He was getting to the part about the protection of God, Divine Love, as he walked through the valley of the shadow of death, when he heard the final call to get out on deck. He grabbed his dressing gown and ran out, sticking the Bible and the *Science and Health* in his pocket.

While the Caldwells were relatively unconcerned a deck below, Beesley and a bunch of men who were congregated on the top deck *were* concerned as they watched the starboard boats being filled with women and children, lowered, and then "rowed away into the darkness." A rumor—it turned out to be unfounded—went around that men were being allowed on lifeboats on the port side. Most of the men, but not Beesley, rushed off in an attempt to find a seat on a lifeboat. Beesley had been looking for his own guardian angel, too, as Christian Science defined angels: "God's thoughts passing to man; spiritual intuitions, pure and perfect." Indeed, Beesley recognized just that sort of guardian angel—a thought, a strong and clear intuition. He felt absolutely certain that he should not follow the other men to the port

*The dapper Reverend William E. Caldwell, Albert's father.*

side. He felt that the divine hand was holding him in place, leading him beside the still waters. It seemed like he was exactly where he was supposed to be. He stayed put.

Meanwhile, Washington Dodge, a first class passenger, was also watching the crew load women and children onto the lifeboats. He had seen his wife and five-year-old son off on Lifeboat 3, but he had stayed behind, obeying the order for women and children to go first. The fact that he had not gotten off the *Titanic* with Mrs. Dodge and little Washington was upsetting to Frederick D. Ray, one of the *Titanic*'s stewards. He was a favorite of the well-traveled Dodge family—so much so that the Dodges had agreed to take the *Titanic* at Ray's urging, specifically to have Ray wait on them. Ray was worried about the Dodges, especially since they were there on his account. Perhaps by now he realized the ship was in serious trouble, which Dodge did not yet really believe. Finally the crew began to launch Lifeboat 13. According to Ray, "They said, 'A few of you men get in here.' There were about nine to a dozen men there, passengers and crew. I saw Mr. Washington Dodge there." Ray asked where Mrs. Dodge and the little boy were, and was relieved to hear they were already on a lifeboat. "He was standing well back from the boat, and I said, 'You had better get in here, then.' I got behind him and pushed him and I followed," Ray recounted before the U.S. Senate Inquiry following the disaster. Ray, who had for so long been something of a guardian angel to the Dodges as they traveled, genuinely became Dodge's guardian angel at that moment, saving his life.

From above, Beesley was still stationed where he thought he ought to be, gazing over the side railing onto the deck below. The sailor loading Lifeboat 13 called for more ladies three times. Seeing none, he looked up and spotted Beesley. "Any ladies on your deck?" he called. Beesley looked around.

"No," he replied. "They were all sent down half an hour ago."

"Then you had better jump," the crewman called. Beesley climbed out on the rail and pushed off, tumbling into Lifeboat 13. He joined Washington Dodge in the boat. There were other men, too, snatched from around the world, including second class men from America and England, plus third class men from Sweden, Ireland, England, Norway, Turkey, and Hong Kong. There was an abundant majority of ladies on the lifeboat, too, who also hailed from various parts of the world, including India, Poland, England, Ireland, Belgium, Sweden, and Canada; and with them were a good number of children.

Meanwhile, Albert was trying to balance the dire picture the stokers painted against the sturdy deck beneath him. Albert apparently protested to one of the stokers that the *Titanic* was so much safer than a lifeboat. It was "so big, and so strongly constructed" that he didn't believe she would sink. Surely she would float for hours, even days. The stoker doggedly offered an alternative, "Get your family off the boat. If it is still here in the morning, you can get back on." Suddenly that made sense to Albert. Many years later, he would look back on that moment and say, "I don't know why I believed him." Then he'd pause and add, "I'll always be thankful for praying parents."

The stoker pointed out Lifeboat 13 right at hand. He sprinted to the gangway door and saw that the boat still had room. He called to the men above who were lowering the boat to hold it. Sylvia and Albert reacted instinctively—the lifeboat had stopped specifically for them, so they dropped all their questions and hurried to it. "And the stokers, about a dozen of 'em, a few other men passengers, my wife, and myself got in boat number 13," Albert summarized years later, thus adding Siam to the worldwide sprinkling of nations represented on Lifeboat 13.

As Beesley recounted in 1912, two latecoming women "tumbled in, [and] the crew shouted, 'Lower away'; but before the order was obeyed, a man with his wife and a baby came quickly to the side: the baby was handed to the lady in the stern, the mother got in near the middle and the father at the last moment dropped in as the boat began its journey down to the sea many feet below." That was Albert, Sylvia, and little Alden.

AS ALBERT TOLD IT a few days after the shipwreck to a reporter who accosted the family en route home to Illinois, "Lifeboat No. 13 was about to be lowered and Mrs. Caldwell was put into it. She was the last woman left in the group, and I was about to lower the baby down to her when she said, 'Can't my husband come, too?' There being ample room I was put into the boat with the baby, and then some other men followed." This account and others like it were important in Albert's story of survival. So many people, for years to come, would hold male survivors in contempt. But accounts of Albert's rescue all depicted him being invited or encouraged by the crew to get onto Lifeboat 13.

Of course, some news stories embellished the scene. A colorful account was printed in the *New York Sun*, enhanced by the reporter's imagination. According to this story, the *Titanic*'s lights went out as the Caldwells made ready to leave their cabin, and they had to feel their way by hearing "shouts and sounds of running. The deck all was chaos. He [Albert] remembers that Mrs. Caldwell got into a lifeboat and he stood by with the baby, crowded away by a swirl of humanity. 'Can't he put the baby in the boat?' his wife shrieked and when he reached over with it some one pushed him and he landed at his wife's feet inside, two other men on top of him." The competing *New York Herald* tried to one-up the rival *Sun* by saying (wrongly) that the Caldwells were thrown from their beds from the "fearful shock" of the collision, and Sylvia, in darkness and confusion that ensued was "suddenly taken and placed into one of the lifeboats." Luckily Albert was somehow able to follow and was trying to hand Alden to her, when she called out, "Can't my husband come aboard with the baby?" The *Herald* said, "Some one behind him shouted 'Sure!' and he was shoved into the boat beside his wife, a couple of other men jumping in on top of him."

The *Washington Post* featured an imaginative scene, worthy of the cover of any modern romance novel. In that account, Sylvia was "one of the prettiest girls in Colorado" and was "said to have been the last woman to leave the sinking *Titanic*." She was indeed pretty, but she wasn't the last woman off, only the last on Lifeboat 13. However, it made for a dramatic story, showcased by a theatrical subheadline: "Mrs. A. F. Caldwell Carried by Husband From *Titanic*." Albert was holding the baby along with his wife in the fanciful story. Albert's romantic gesture, the newspaper said, saved his life because it won him a spot in the lifeboat. In fact, the newspaper's headline set forth the myth that Albert and all male survivors would fight the rest of their lives by suggesting that men were not normally allowed off the ship. The headline blared dramatically, "WIFE AS HIS PASSPORT."

Significantly, the Caldwells' exit from the *Titanic* seemed to vindicate Dr. Walker's diagnosis of Sylvia many months earlier. Some of the missionaries thought Sylvia was merely suffering from the aftermath of pregnancy or even hypochondria, or was not suffering from anything except a bought-and-paid-for diagnosis. However, the *Titanic* belied that condemnation. If you read between the lines, you can guess that Sylvia had a condition that was apparent to the naked eye—such as weakened arms, a bent back, or limping legs—and that prevented her from holding Alden.

A visible symptom is suggested in the account by Hilda Slayter of the steward who tried to take Alden out of Albert's arms. Hilda told the steward there were no more women coming, and the man then let Albert go through the checkpoint. Given that some of the policemen-like bedroom stewards reportedly "let out their fists at one or two men who attempted to get into the boats," Hilda's request was not necessarily one that they would have approved. Why would the crewman break the "women and children" rule that he was striving so hard to enforce, to the point of grabbing the baby by force from his father? Perhaps Hilda was just that persuasive. Or perhaps it was obvious to the steward, when Hilda directed his attention to the problem, that Albert was indeed needed to hold the baby because something was visibly wrong with Sylvia.

Over many years, Sylvia and Albert were remarkably consistent in admitting that Albert had to hold the baby, a fact they made neither apology nor explanation for. Over the next couple of decades, this unusual reversal of parenting duties (especially in regards to the "women and children first" atmosphere on the *Titanic*) was featured in their descriptions of that awful night, again hinting that something was wrong with Sylvia.

Albert described it this way in the *Park College Alumniad* magazine in April, 1912: "I owe my life to my baby boy or rather to God who used him to save me. The fact that I had him in my arms gave me precedence to take a vacant place in the life-boat after the women and children were loaded." About two weeks after that, a reporter said that Sylvia got into the lifeboat, and then, "seeing no other ladies, Mr. Caldwell with babe in arms stepped into the boat . . . He says his life was saved because of the child in his arms." Both accounts implied that he was needed to hold the baby; the thought of handing the baby to Sylvia just didn't seem to occur to her, him, or officials standing by.

Interestingly, the *Washington Post* said outright that Sylvia was ill. The article intoned dramatically in bold type, "Her Illness Saved Mate," following that with, "She was ill on board the *Titanic* at the time of the disaster, and to her indisposition and weakness her husband, who was accompanying her home, owes his life, for he was allowed to take her and the child in his arms into the last lifeboat."

ALTHOUGH ALBERT WAS SAFELY now in the lifeboat, "safe" was no one's adjective of choice at the moment. As Sylvia told it, "It seemed that fate toyed with our lives all thru that awful night, a succession of narrow escapes from death coming in rapid sequences." The lifeboat jerked down toward the water at uneven angles, tipping forward and then backward. Sylvia said dramatically that they had to hold onto the sides of the boat to keep from being pitched out. Then they had to contend with water pouring from the *Titanic*'s condenser pumps, gushing in a forceful stream three or four feet in diameter right in the path of Lifeboat 13. Washington Dodge was sure they would be swamped by it. Everyone began screaming to the crew to stop lowering, and they frantically tried to locate the oars to push the boat away from the ship. The oars were lashed tightly to the lifeboat's side with twine—and people were sitting on them besides—so the task was none too easy. The cascading water created a freezing spray. By the time Lifeboat 13 struck the Atlantic, at least some of the passengers were quite wet. Given the nearly unbearable temperature, it was a miracle, Sylvia thought, that the Caldwells didn't so much as catch cold.

And then the confounded mechanical parts of the lifeboat did not work as expected. As Albert described it many years later, "When we got down to the water, we couldn't get loose from the block and tackle. There was a lever at the center of the boat that was supposed to pull to loosen the block and tackle, but it was all gummed up with paint." Beesley described a pin to be released, rather than a lever. Whether lever or pin, Albert indicated paint as the culprit in jamming the equipment. As he recalled it, a thickened layer of red paint paralyzed the apparatus. The *Titanic* was a new ship, after all, and the paint had not had time to wear down. And clearly no one had bothered to test the lifesaving equipment. Walter Williams, a second class steward who wound up on Lifeboat 13, had been surprised during the all-too-short voyage that there had been no lifeboat drill, and he could confirm the paint issue. When he came aboard, the paint was so new that it was still wet on his locker. It's perhaps no surprise, then, that paint had pooled where it was not meant to.

Meanwhile, Lifeboat 15 was being lowered, and Lifeboat 13 was directly beneath it, having been pushed under it in the frenzied effort to avoid the roaring water from the condenser pumps. This was quite alarming. Everyone on 13 was yelling for the men lowering the boats to stop, but 15 kept coming. No one could hear them over the roar of the water. Fifteen "would have crushed us and all would have been lost," Sylvia said, recalling the terror of seeing the bottom of 15 coming far too close. People reached up with their hands on the bottom of 15 in a futile gesture to stop it as others tried frantically to release 13 by the jammed mechanism. At first the crewmen lowering 15 were "heedless of our shrieks and terror," as Albert put it. But then, thankfully, "the men above realized what was happening, and they held the boat over our heads," he recalled.

For the second time that night, a stoker played guardian angel to the Caldwell family—and this time, to everyone on Lifeboat 13. Stoker Frederick Barrett and an able seaman, Robert Hopkins, took out knives—Sylvia thought one of the knives was handed down from 15—and sawed away at the ropes that still stubbornly bound 13 to the *Titanic*. Barrett had to tread across several women in the boat to get to the ropes, but in the moment of crisis, no one complained. At last, 13 was set free. Relieved, Sylvia noted that the boat "slid away in the nick of time, another perilous escape."

No one was officially designated to be in' charge, but the people on Lifeboat 13 felt they needed a leader. "We elected one of the stokers to be our captain," Albert said, recalling him as a "jolly" man. The stoker was Barrett, who had already meant so much to the Caldwells. He had possibly helped Albert get his photo shoveling coal (the camera, alas, having been left behind ); he may well have been the one who pleaded with Albert to get off the ship; he had severed the stuck ropes that tied 13 hazardously to the *Titanic*. Now Barrett apparently tried to keep everyone's spirits up with a cheerful demeanor. He didn't know what else to do; this sudden promotion to captain of this tiny vessel under the most horrible of circumstances might be his first and last command. He was doing his best to make the catastrophe bearable. "He gave direction to us men as we rowed about, trying to keep up with the other boats," Albert said.

The crewmen aboard Lifeboat 13 had been directed to row toward the lights of the ship they could see in the distance, and seaman Hopkins reported that they earnestly tried to get there, but the light moved away and disappeared. Despite the crewmen's well-meaning efforts at rowing, Dodge observed that they weren't too good at it. "Those who undertook to handle the oars were poor oarsmen, almost without exception, and our progress was extremely slow," he said. Mary Hewlett, also on 13, agreed. She criticized later, "Then we pulled out from the *Titanic* somehow as the men at the oars did not know how to row—could not keep time & did not know starboard from port!!!" As Beesley put it, "All night long their oars crossed and clashed; if our safety had depended on speed or accuracy in keeping time it would have gone hard with us." Perhaps the stokers who were rowing could be forgiven that shortcoming. They were dressed lightly to work amongst the hot furnaces, and some had gotten wet as the *Titanic* flooded below. In their damp condition in the excruciating cold, they were freezing. Ruth Becker, the twelve-year-old daughter of a missionary family leaving India, came to their rescue. As the *Titanic*'s lifeboats were being loaded, Ruth clutched blankets meant for her siblings. Crewmen put the younger Beckers onto Lifeboat 11 and announced it was full. Mrs. Becker pleaded to go with them. The crew let her on, but began lowering the lifeboat without Ruth. Mrs. Becker called out to Ruth to get another boat, and she was relieved to witness Ruth placed into Lifeboat 13. Throughout all of this trauma, Ruth had not let go of the blankets. "Stokers were row-ing the boats and they just had sleeveless shirts and shorts, because it's so hot down there in the engine room," Ruth recalled. "The officer asked if I would give up my blankets to put around the stokers to keep them halfway warm, and then of course rowing the boat, now that kept them warm too." She passed the blankets out to the half-frozen men. Hilda Slayter, who had extra coats with her, gave those out as well. Steward Frederick Ray passed out handkerchiefs to six shivering people, and they twisted the corners into knots to warm their bare heads. Numbed through but warming up at last in Ruth's blanket, Barrett turned the tiller over to someone else and fell asleep.

To help relieve the troubled rowers, Albert took one of the six oars. It was not until they had rowed a good distance from the ship—maybe half a mile, to avoid the suction that the ship would generate if it sank —that Albert looked up and was startled to see that the *Titanic* really was going down. The rows of portholes, which should have been parallel to the water, slid in a sickening procession into the Atlantic, burning onward in a hor-rible glow underneath the surface. "That was the first time I believed she would sink," Albert admitted. Others on 13 were just as startled to realize the *Titanic* really was sinking. As the still-blazing portholes settled lower, the ocean swallowed them whole, like a drinker of flaming raisins in flap-dragon, the cruel game used as a metaphor for a shipwreck in the lines spoken by Albert's character, the Clown, in Park College's performance of *The Winter's Tale*. Shakespeare's picture was eerily prescient. As the Atlantic played out its sinister version of flap-dragon, the *Titanic* had by then about half an hour left, and this was the first Albert was aware of it. There had been no panic, no stumbling on a sloping deck, no reason to believe the ship was so fatally wounded until now. Had the stoker not warned him about the danger, he and his family would still be aboard. Had Albert not been posing for a picture with the stokers earlier in the voyage, the stoker would not have singled him out to convince him to get off the ship.

The occupants of Lifeboat 13 watched the *Titanic* as she settled lower and lower into the water, a chilling, surreal spectacle. By now Alden was in the arms of Hilda Slayter, whose quick thinking had gotten Albert past the grim bedroom stewards. Alden had slept quietly in her arms for some time, when he woke up and began to cry. It was too dark to see anything and too tight to move around to maneuver the baby. Hilda asked Lawrence Beesley, whom she could just make out in the dark beside her, "Will you feel down and see if the baby's feet are out of the blanket? I don't know much about babies but I think their feet must be kept warm."

Beesley was startled to recognize her voice. He had sat at dinner with her on the voyage. He asked, "Surely you are Miss Slayter?" She responded, "Yes, and you must be Mr. Beesley; how curious we should find ourselves on the same boat!"

Beesley wriggled around and found Alden's "toes exposed to the air and wrapped them well up, when it ceased crying at once; it was evidently a successful diagnosis!" If Alden had indeed been wearing his soft little baby shoes off the ship, he had kicked them off. The blanket satisfied him, and he blissfully fell back to sleep, warm in Hilda's arms and keeping Hilda toasty as well.

Interestingly, Albert and Sylvia avoided mentioning in newspaper interviews that strangers held their beloved infant on the lifeboat. Sylvia did refer to it in a private letter to *Titanic* historian Walter Lord in his research for the book *A Night to Remember* in 1955, saying that Lawrence Beesley held the baby. She mentioned Alden crying about his cold feet in a Colorado interview in 1912, but she didn't add that she wasn't holding him. For her part on April 15, 1912, probably Sylvia was too weak or too seasick to care who was holding Alden—she was probably grateful that someone was keeping him out of harm's way, as she was not up to it. It seems likely, in fact, that Alden was passed hand to hand. In a speech right after the disaster, Albert said that he got into 13, hugging Alden tightly. He ducked to the bottom of the lifeboat to keep the baby warm and out of the wind. In a different version, Steward Ray told of a bundle thrown "about 2 or 3 feet to me, and I caught it, and unrolled the blankets, and found that it was a little baby." According to one source, Ray called out, "Who'll take this babby?" and passed "babby" Alden to a young woman who volunteered—but not to his mother.

That volunteer may well have passed the baby back to Albert after he was in place. Albert was soon asked to row, and he would have passed the baby to someone else—probably to Hilda Slayter. The various nannies to Alden once again vindicated Dr. Walker's opinion on Sylvia's condition. Ray, in catching "babby" Alden, did not hesitate to ask for volunteers to hold the baby, even though he said outright that he saw the mother approach. Apparently, he could tell something was wrong with Sylvia and deemed her unable to hold Alden. Hilda Slayter, when she finally wound up with Alden, evidently didn't question holding him or call out to locate the mother. She apparently already knew the mother was not able to hold him. If members of the Foreign Missions Board needed convincing that Sylvia was truly unwell, they should have been on Lifeboat 13 that night.

BUT THE CALDWELLS' TROUBLES with the Foreign Missions Board seemed remote and unimportant as 13 struggled farther away from the injured *Titanic*. The refugees in the lifeboat all had their eyes on the ship. Her lights burned until a few minutes before she sank—about ten minutes, Albert guessed. Suddenly there was a horrible noise. "We distinctly heard the sound of the boilers exploding" on the *Titanic*, Albert said, "and then the bow of the steamer sank from view." Without electricity and without her bow, the *Titanic* was only a wounded blot standing at about 45 degrees against the brightly unconcerned stars. The last Albert saw of the *Titanic* was "the stern of the boat outlined against the starry sky. And then with a gentle swish, she disappeared from sight."

Everyone was stunned that the *Titanic* was really gone. Sylvia described the moment as "fantastic with horror." There they sat in the terrible flatness of the sea, a "vast waste of water," as Albert saw it, without the majestic *Titanic* to compete with the incongruously cheerful starlight. For a minute everything was quiet, holding its collective breath in ghastly silence. And then the cries started. As Sylvia described it, "The huge, almost defying [defying God, that is] work of man had dived to it's grave. There was no sound but the dip of the oars in the water. When suddenly there arose upon the stillness, the weirdest, most appalling, heart rending noise that ever mortal might hear—the cry of hundreds of human souls for help." It was awful. "Pity them who could not be saved," she mourned, and then added herself and Albert and all the other survivors into the sad equation: "Aye and pity those who heard them and could not save them." A man in Lifeboat 13 suggested that the people in the water were singing, "but who could be deceived?" Sylvia said sorrowfully.

Others on 13 *wanted* to be deceived. They asserted that people in various lifeboats were merely calling to each other. But it was not so. Indeed, as Sylvia said, who could be deceived by such wishful thinking? Sylvia herself believed with anguish that many of the *Titanic's* victims "drowned like rats in a trap," having never been awakened from their beds. "Icy water soon benumbed those who were left behind and they sank, to rise no more," she said.

Albert would say in later years, "You just have to forget the screams, or you'd go crazy."

But there was no forgetting them now. Someone in the dark lifeboat suggested that they sing, and a quavering female voice started a song. Sylvia recalled it as a hymn, but Elizabeth Dowdell on their boat remembered it as "We Parted on the Shore," a shanty with despondent lyrics that mourned, in part:

> Now it's years and years . . .
> Since I left my bonny lassie on the shore.
> I never will forget that day; she cried so many tears.
> I'd never seen so many tears before!
> . . . And when I saw that, we parted on the shore.

To Sylvia, it was the ultimate bravery. "In her effort to comfort and keep from our ears those pitiful cries, she offered her mite of cheer," Sylvia said. "Can you picture the scene? In the middle of the Atlantic ocean, in the darkness of the night, out in that mighty deep, in a boat that a wave could crush; one woman's voice going up in song while the poor quavering voice was almost drowned by the voice of the perishing."

Albert thought of the church service they had attended only a short time earlier in the *Titanic*'s second class dining room. "How little did those who were worshipping God at that time realize that, within a few hours, the majority of them would meet Him," he reflected.

Albert was aghast about that watertight door that had not been closed. For years he would believe that the watertight doors had not been closed at all, and had the captain closed them, the ship would not have sunk. He didn't realize that the *Titanic* was so badly damaged by the iceberg that she never really had a chance. At that moment in 1912, it appeared to him and the other survivors that the watertight doors had tragically not performed in the way they had been hyped. "We all thought the boat non-sinkable and I believe that the poor fellows who were lost had hope to the end that she would not sink for many hours," he told his college alumni magazine half a month later. Indeed, that stoker's insistence that the *Titanic would* sink had truly meant the world to the Caldwells.

The catastrophic outcome of that overconfidence in technology spread bleak and cold before them. The bitter air nipped sharply at exposed faces, hands, Alden's toes. As Albert noted drearily, "We didn't know when help would come." *If* it would come, he might have said. They couldn't find a light on their lifeboat, nor could they find any water to drink nor food to eat. It was a stark, terrifying contrast from the lavish *Titanic*, where they had chosen from the huge menu of delicacies just a few hours earlier.

THE GNAWING COLD PARTICULARLY mocked the Caldwells. Sylvia had suffered so in the tropics. They had fled from the sultry, health-sucking heat of Siam in hopes that a cooler climate would restore Sylvia's health. They had risked their good names and their carefully secreted savings to get to that fresher, more northerly climate against the wishes of many important people whom they worked with and respected, the people who had been their friends and colleagues their entire married life. And now Albert and Sylvia found the stark opposite of Siam, a cold so dense that it was killing people right there as they listened, torturing the living with the fact that they could not help—and with the fact that the lack of help was fatal.

The Caldwells had weighed their options and had deemed it worthwhile to risk their reputations and their life savings in an effort to save Sylvia's bodily health and sanity. Now their life savings were gone and their lives were grimly at risk. Just six inches from the water in a nearly swamped row-boat, they were only one mishap removed from joining the poor, freezing souls clinging to floating pieces of the wreckage, whose cries were growing thinner and rarer as they lapsed into unconsciousness and then froze. After about an hour, the cries died out altogether in a chilling, finalized silence.

It was easy to see that their own lot was nearly as dire. If no one knew they were out there on the Atlantic, how would they ever be found? No food, no fresh water, freezing temperatures—and Alden dressed so scantily in a sleeper and surely by now a very wet diaper, with his little shoes (if he had been wearing them) kicked off in the wet bottom of the lifeboat—and no real sense of whether rescue was at hand. There was nothing to do but wait in agonizing worry. Someone on Lifeboat 13 said grimly, "This is no joke; we may knock about here days before we are picked up, if at all." Washington Dodge thought everyone was depressed. At one point they were startled to spot a sailing ship close at hand. Could they be saved? As they rowed closer, they found that it was a small iceberg.

There were so many stars that night—constellations twinkled in their blazing glory, unobscured in the otherwise black world. It would have been pretty had the circumstances been different. Possibly Albert's thoughts wandered to his high school graduation oration, "Night Brings Forth the Stars." It was discouragingly paradoxical that his launch into the world, heralded with his self-chosen metaphor of stars, might end so appallingly here under them.

One of the evacuees on 13 was one of the *Titanic*'s lookouts, Reginald Lee. He told Sylvia that he had seen mist in the ship's path and had warned the bridge that he thought they were heading into ice. Not that he had any binoculars to check the mist better, as he wished he did. The bridge disregarded his warning. In fact, he said, he had warned the bridge three times about ice, and finally on the third warning the first officer, who had the bridge, at last changed course. The revelation was shocking. Albert associated the information with the *Titanic*'s goal of a fast crossing and would afterward complain that the boat sank because of sheer carelessness, which included speeding through the ice field. As one reporter summed up Albert's comments later, "No heed was given to the warning, and the big ocean greyhound plunged ahead to her doom simply to gratify the demand that she break all records."

Now they were out in the North Atlantic with a miserable truth tyrannizing them: chances seemed quite good, as had been the case for millennia, that they had only prolonged an inevitable death by managing to escape on a lifeboat. The tiny lifeboat fleet, all that remained of the biggest ship on the ocean, was alone and very small in the dark.

Would any ship ever be able to find them?

# 7

# Pull for the Shore, Sailor

The castaways shivered in the blackness of the thankfully calm Atlantic, waiting for . . . well, they *hoped* they were waiting for rescue. The *Titanic* had gone down at 2:20 A.M., and there were the unforgettable screams, and finally the quiet and hideous contemplation of what had just happened—and what might happen to them.

Conditions were not good, given the lack of light, food, water, rescue. The one thing they had in their favor was a calm sea. The Atlantic, Albert noted, was always rough, but not this one night. It was calmer than a lake. Young Ruth Becker thought it was like taking a boat ride on a mill pond.

Several of the refugees in Lifeboat 13 tried to prop up sagging spirits by assuring everyone that they had been told four or five steamers had been summoned and were on the way. Beesley recalled that people put great hope on the thought that the *Olympic* would be there by 2 P.M., based on crewmen's calculations. As Beesley saw it, everyone was confident they would be rescued. One of the stokers predicted, "The sea will be covered with ships tomorrow afternoon: they will race up from all over the sea to find us."

And yet there was that disheartening memory of the ship whose lights they could all see from the *Titanic* while she still floated, and it never came. There was also the light they had tried to row to, but it had disappeared. *Nothing* could really be sure, and this nagging doubt loomed behind any optimism about rescue. As Dodge noted, "Every pair of eyes were strained to the utmost, to discover the first sign of approaching help." Mary Hewlett fished out letters to her daughters from her handbag, and someone set them afire one by one to provide a light. A few of the lifeboats had lanterns, and others burned paper, too, and "these facts led several in our boat to assert many times, that they saw a new light, which certainly must be a steamer's light," Dodge said. So many times their hopes were swallowed as cruelly as the *Titanic* had been. "With each disappointment, added gloom seemed to settle upon our little company, as they began to realize the seriousness of our situation," Dodge recalled. Percy Thomas Oxenham reckoned that the five and a half hours adrift in doubt and darkness "were the most awful [hours] I ever put in."

Around an hour after the *Titanic* had disappeared, someone on 13 said he could see a light glowing up from the horizon—it seemed low and man-made. The other survivors did not dare believe it at first. "No one . . . placed any credence in his statement," Dodge noted; the glow looked at that moment like some of the other discouraging lights they had chased already. At first Albert thought it was an optical illusion, or he was afraid it would be, anyway, and he strained to see it again. However, shortly the sharp-eyed passenger could see two lights, and then even Dodge could discern one. Albert could tell it wasn't a star or a planet, and it certainly wasn't the dawn. Then suddenly he was sure: it was a light—a wavering light, a faint beam of hope! Everyone's skepticism dwindled as the light grew brighter, until even the most pessimistic were rejoicing. Someone *had* known where they were! Someone *was* coming to their rescue! Suddenly there was something else to think about besides the cries of gruesome death they had just heard. There was sincere optimism that they might live through this terrible night. Their eyes fixed on the wavering beam. It got brighter and brighter, little by little, clearly coming toward them. After some time, as dawn approached, they could just make out the mast of a steamer. The refugees on 13 were thrilled but worried about being run down by their heroic rescuer. Their little boat was so dark. They managed to twist more letters into a torch and set fire to it, a stoker waving it aloft. "We were quite prepared to burn our coats if necessary," Beesley said.

As the ship came into plain view, the men on 13 chorused into a ragged version of "Pull for the Shore, Sailor." The words were well suited to their surging relief:

> Light in the darkness, sailor, day is at hand! . . .
> Drear was the voyage, sailor, now almost o'er,

Safe within the life boat, sailor, pull for the shore.

Pull for the shore, sailor, pull for the shore!
Heed not the rolling waves, but bend to the oar;
Safe in the life boat, sailor, cling to self no more!
Leave the poor old stranded wreck, and pull for the shore.

As Beesley noted, the quaveringly grateful singers on Lifeboat 13 were too overwhelmed to sing properly, so they tried a cheer, shouting out praise for Guglielmo Marconi for inventing the wireless, which had summoned their rescuer. No doubt the wobbly song and stronger cheer helped rouse them for the final difficult push, as the rescue ship had stopped some distance away. It was a tall order for the half-frozen men to row—they even had to row around a berg. Nor was the rowing easy; Oxenham, a strong stone cutter at age twenty-two, admitted, "When the *Carpathia* hove into sight nearly everyone in our boat was exhausted."

But no one was focusing on the freezing weather or fatigue any longer. Men and women alike were crying "tears of joy mingled with tears of sorrow," Sylvia reported. Dawn bloomed full and fresh into a rosy sky, revealing the rescue ship carefully stopped among the dreadful ice. "Never was dawn more welcome," Sylvia said gratefully. Albert was startled to see all the ice around—and to see that it was beautiful. The ice was so harmless-looking. And the ice had in fact changed its cruel face to benevolence; after crushing the *Titanic*, the ice had surrounded the desperate flotilla of lifeboats and had protected them in the calm sea between bergs. Without that ironic protection, the nearly swamped lifeboats might have been overturned into the normally choppy Atlantic, which was actually colder than ice. In fact, that swath of ocean would have been frozen that night save for its salt content; its temperature was well below 32 degrees.

Lifeboat 13 was among the first to reach the rescue ship. As the light mustered itself into a true morning, Albert was startled to recognize the ship. It was the *Carpathia*, which they had spotted in Naples! She was on her return voyage to the Mediterranean, in fact. It was a remarkable turn-around in perspective—the Caldwells had flirted with the idea of taking the *Carpathia* in March, but had turned her down because she was a little ship. Now she looked so huge against the tiny lifeboat. The day Albert and Sylvia had looked at the *Carpathia* in Naples seemed long, long ago now, not just a few short weeks. Whole lifetimes had passed last night, after all.

Now, Sylvia and Albert, like everyone else, were deeply thankful to be unexpectedly added to the *Carpathia's* passenger list. Her crew threw down a rope ladder, but things were getting tricky. As the sun came up, so did the wind, and the ocean was getting rough. "Our boat seemed longing to leave the side of the ship," Sylvia noted. The danger, so close to safety, clutched everyone. Perhaps the motion was also enough to induce queasiness in Sylvia. She couldn't climb the rope ladder due to the sheer cold, the rough seas, or her ongoing illness, so she sat on a rope swing and was pulled up. Some of the other women got the same treatment. The *Carpathia's* crew lowered a sack for baby Alden, now in his daddy's arms again. Albert stuffed Alden into the sack and watched his precious baby hoisted up the steep side of the *Carpathia*. The men, including Albert, scrambled up rope ladders.

Sylvia stumbled onto the *Carpathia* with her teeth chattering, numbed through. It was obvious that the crew had been up all night, waiting for them; the crew was nearing exhaustion. Sylvia tried to stammer out her appreciation to the *Carpathia* sailors who had pulled her up onto the ship. "Oh, thank you!" she managed.

"Don't stop for that, we are only too happy to be here to do it," one replied. Sylvia couldn't walk—perhaps because her mysterious symptoms affected her feet or legs. Then again, maybe she was just too frozen. She had to be carried to the dining room, where she was given hot coffee and brandy, which was more a medication at that moment than a liquor. As the crewman placed her in a chair, Sylvia noted sadly the "sorry sight." There were women all around the table, "wild eyed and haggard silently weeping." Most were wearing nightgowns; they had not even managed to escape the *Titanic* with modest or warm clothing. Their hair was not put up as fashion demanded; it streamed down their backs. A foreign woman was calling out frantically for her baby. That was the only noise, other than sobbing, and

Sylvia recognized the sobs as a release for so many of the women.

After warming up in the *Carpathia*'s dining room, the Caldwells moved to the deck to watch as the other lifeboats rowed toward the *Carpathia*. They sat together in stunned silence, a rare *Titanic* family. At first during the darkness they had thought that perhaps forty or fifty heroic crewmen who had remained aboard the sinking ship had been crying for help from the icy waters. Now they could see that they had grossly underestimated. The Caldwells didn't know how many of their fellow passengers had been lost, but it quickly became obvious that they were one of the few families who had started out together on the *Titanic*'s short voyage and had completed it together. Counting parents traveling with children, couples traveling without children, and siblings traveling without parents, only one family in four who got onto the *Titanic* together got off together. More than seventy families vanished entirely.

The survival of all three of the Caldwells was their own miracle amidst so much heartbreaking tragedy, a miracle they could not celebrate except with subdued reverence. Sylvia told a reporter some time afterward, "As I look back over the perils of that fearful night, it seems miraculous that all three of us are yet together. The margin between life and death was so narrow." So many people had lost a loved one or multiple loved ones. She noticed with dismay the scene repeated over and over among the *Titanic*'s surviving women: "A life boat would come up and the eager, half frozen wives and mothers stood and scanned the faces of those entering; another boat and those poor, wild eyes, never tireing, searched in vain." Albert, too, was deeply saddened to watch the *Titanic*'s women who lined the rails of the *Carpathia*, scanning each incoming lifeboat "in the vain hope of seeing a husband, a father, a brother or perhaps a sweetheart who never came." A rumor went around that some survivors had been picked up by another ship. Women who had yet to locate their husbands were on a roller coaster ride between utter despair and desperate hope.

And yet it always turned out to be hope toying with them in the most merciless way. One of the women searching in vain was the Caldwells' *Titanic* dinner companion, Lottie Collyer. "We could only rush frantically from group to group, searching the haggard faces, crying out names, and endless questions," Mrs. Collyer recalled later. "No survivor knows better than I the bitter cruelty of disappointment and despair. I had a husband to search for, a husband whom in the greatness of my faith, I had believed would be found in one of the boats. He was not there."

Captain Arthur Henry Rostron of the *Carpathia* had his wireless radio operator contact all ships in the vicinity, but the gravely final word came back, "We have no survivors." Someone on the *Carpathia* began the bleak task of counting the *Titanic*'s passengers on board. "We knew then, after being counted, that 1,500 had been lost," Albert said. And yet here they were, the intact Caldwell family, a gift of God—and of their guardian angel, that persistent stoker who had insisted they get off the *Titanic*. Gratefully, Albert asked to see the crewmen who had manned 13. He thanked them, particularly the stoker who had told them the raw truth about the damage to the *Titanic*.

It looked to Albert as though the *Carpathia* was full up, and conditions were crowded. There was plenty of food, "although it was a task [for the *Carpathia*'s kitchen staff] to cook quickly for such a large number" Albert commented. The *Carpathia* had been heading back to the Mediterranean, but Captain Rostron canceled that schedule and return to New York. The rescue ship turned around mid-day, and Albert "looked back at the great ice field with the great icebergs glistening in the noon day sun. They looked so beautiful and harmless." But he sighed. Looks were cruelly deceiving. The proud *Titanic* lay at the bottom of the ocean, having taken with her "millions of dollars worth of property and hundreds of precious lives, having been crushed by one of those harmless looking objects."

After a few hours Sylvia was sitting to one side with Alden on her lap. One of the *Titanic* stewards came by. He picked up Alden and hugged him tightly, tears welling up in his eyes. He didn't say a word at first. Then, as Sylvia told it, "He put my babe in his arms, sat down by my side and said, 'I have a son at home, just the age of this little fellow and I never saw two babies more alike.'" Both babies were lucky to still have fathers.

Albert's own good fortune was brutally clear: he watched the *Carpathia*'s crew bury some of the *Titanic*'s men at sea. They had managed to swim to a lifeboat, but the *Carpathia* was too late to keep the soaked men from freezing to death. He spoke with one survivor who *had* made it through after swimming.

As the Caldwells quickly realized, most of the new widows aboard were immigrating to America, having never been there before. Sylvia eavesdropped on their conversations as they talked at the dining room tables or in corners where they were huddled. She overheard one say, "I have nothing in the world and I have no place to go since my husband is lost. But I am not afraid. I have always heard that the Americans were the kindest people in the world." Sylvia sat up a little straighter at the compliment to her country that she herself had been gone from for such a significant time in her life that it seemed like another world. When she was last a resident of America in 1909, she was the daughter of her parents, a Harbaugh. Now she was a married former missionary with a husband and a child, a Caldwell with a son of her own. Another woman turned to Sylvia and said, "Now I am not saying this because you are an American; but some how I feel as if I were going to friends. I have never been to America but I would rather it was America I was going to, in this condition than any other country in the world." Another snatch of conversation Sylvia overheard featured a woman worrying what would become of her family. A friend tried to comfort her. "Never mind, I never saw an American who didn't have a big heart," her companion said. "I am sure they will take good care of us." As Sylvia said, "I think I was never so proud that I was American as then."

For their part, the people on the *Carpathia* were certainly good to the shocked and bereaved survivors. A lady tore up her flannel nightgown to make diapers for babies; no doubt Alden was the recipient of this desperately needed generosity. Fellow *Titanic* survivor Margaret "Molly" Brown, the well-known Denver millionaire, took charge of the women aboard the *Carpathia*, including the *Titanic's* own women, and organized them into a team to replace the clothes of children who by now had soiled, spit up on, spilled on, or in other ways dirtied their clothing. Molly Brown and the ladies appropriated the *Carpathia's* steamer rugs and made them into poncho-like dresses or coats for the little ones. Alden really needed a coat; some stranger had made a souvenir of at least one of the *Titanic's* steamer rugs that he had been swaddled in when the *Carpathia* crew hoisted him from the lifeboat. Molly Brown brought a homemade coat to little Alden personally. Sylvia's parents lived in Colorado, so perhaps Sylvia was bold enough to speak of home with Mrs. Brown.

Alden looked like an urchin in his strange garment, and technically, he *was*. The Caldwells had lost every material thing they had owned, although material things seemed paltry at the moment compared to the profound losses suffered by the widows and bereaved mothers and orphaned daughters who were all around them in shock, tears, or both. The Caldwells didn't complain about the strange garment and gratefully let Alden wear it. It was no doubt heady to have rubbed elbows with Molly Brown as well. Sylvia was well aware of social status, and meeting the famous Mrs. Brown was something the Caldwells would never forget.

Thinking of the gold and jewelry she and Albert had left in their trunk, Sylvia noted that few of the *Titanic's* women now aboard the *Carpathia* had any money on them, and those who did had only a little. "Nevertheless," she said, "I saw women who had but five dollars [$110 today] themselves, all they owned in the world, going around and buying for those who had not a cent." Toothbrushes sold out right away, noted Mary Hewlett.

The *Titanic's* survivors had to be organized on the *Carpathia* to fit everyone in. That night women with babies, Sylvia and little Alden included, were given blankets so they could sleep on the floor of the dining room. That arrangement continued for the next three nights, although it was none too restful. They had to get up at 5:30 A.M. so that the *Carpathia's* crew could ready the dining area for breakfast. Sylvia didn't complain, however, and neither did the other mothers on the dining room floor. "Always I saw the tired, heavy hearted rise, most of them with a smile," Sylvia marveled.

The women on the *Carpathia* "gave away all the clothing they could spare and more too," Sylvia noticed. One gave soap, hair pins "and [found] the mother with the suckling child and to her she would give fruit and milk." Perhaps this was Sylvia herself, as Alden was one of the youngest survivors. "The hearts of humanity were opened," Sylvia noticed. Then, casting her missionary's eye on the situation, she added, "God was working in a mysterious way."

Albert "camp[ed] in a chair and got what sleep I could," he recalled, which was not too much. To while away time, he picked up a pen and wrote a letter to someone who was on his mind: Dr. C. C. Walker back in Bangkok. It was Walker who had ordered Sylvia home against the opinion of the chairman of the mission, R. C. Jones, and four others. Walker had been a true friend to the Caldwells, despite the predicament they now faced. Albert wrote:

Royal Mail Steamship *Carpathia*
Dear Folks,

Here we are safe. We were one of few families who kept together when the *Titanic* went down. Hundreds of lives were lost, mostly men. Nearly all the women and children were saved. The trouble was, no one realized the danger, and thought this "largest boat in the world" would not sink, and if she did it would take many hours.

She struck the iceberg at midnight and in a little over two hours she was at the bottom.

We were picked up by this boat at daylight. The ocean was as calm as a lake, while we were in the life boats.

As the people did not realize how quick she would go down, there was no hurry and the life boats were not full enough. Some of the boats went down with the ship and there were not enough boats in the first place. The *Titanic* was considered a "non-sinkable" boat.

We were 1500 miles from New York. This boat was bound for Gibraltar when she picked us up, but she turned around and is taking us to New York.

I understand that about 700 were saved. There are many, many wives who have lost their husbands.

We are very very thankful to God for his "Goodness" to us and know that it was the prayers of our loved ones and friends that saved us.

It was a sad sight to see that beautiful ship go down and awful to hear the shrieks of the hundreds who were dying.

It was a terrible night and one that I will never forget.

The names of the survivors were sent to N.Y. so we hope that our folks

have heard of our safety, as they knew we were on the *Titanic*.
    Address us
    c/o Rev. W. E. Caldwell
    Biggsville,
    Ill.
    Sylvia and Alden are well and we are so happy & thankful.
    Yours Sincerely,
    A. F. Caldwell

The letter was powerful in its simplicity, the stark first retelling by Albert of a story he would repeat over and over again for the next sixty-five years. Interestingly, he identified Sylvia as being well, no doubt a reference to the fact that she had escaped the wreck, but also unconsciously pointing out why R. C. Jones had insisted on a medical examination for Sylvia behind the Caldwells' backs. One wonders today if the "Folks" to whom the letter was addressed meant *all* of the missionaries (Jones included) or only Dr. Walker and his wife.

**BACK IN THE STATES,** the Caldwells' family had *not* heard they were saved. Albert's cousin, Dr. Charles Swan Caldwell, told the *Pittsburgh Post* that he feared his cousin and wife had not survived. William and Fannie Caldwell, frantically scanning their local newspaper on April 16, were horrified to see their son's name was not on the "saved" list, nor was Sylvia's name nor baby Alden's. But it was only a partial list. They got back down on their knees, not knowing if they were praying for the living or the dead. The next day, thank God, Albert, Sylvia, and Alden appeared in the list of those saved. Meanwhile, Sylvia's mother had no idea they were on the *Titanic* until she saw an "A. Caldwell" on a list of people saved. It "awakened the anxiety of Mrs. Harbaugh for a short time, [but] she soon dismissed the idea of her daughter or son-in-law being on the ship," a Colorado newspaper reported. Mrs. Harbaugh found out the startling news that "A. Caldwell" really did refer to her family when she got a cablegram from Sylvia saying they had been picked up by the *Carpathia* and had arrived safely in New York.

The relatives weren't the only ones who were anxiously reading the lists of survivors. Numerous Park College graduates lived in New York, and more were attending a Conservation Congress meeting in town. Word spread amongst them like a Missouri prairie fire—the Caldwells were among the saved and were headed back to New York via the *Carpathia*. They probably found out the Caldwells had been on the *Titanic* through H. B. McAfee, the treasurer of Park College himself, who was in town. McAfee's brother Cleland was on the Presbyterian Board of Foreign Missions, and Cleland probably knew what ship the Caldwells were on, since the Board was supposed to pay for their transportation. It would have been easy for Cleland to tell H. B. about the Park grads' rescue. H. B. McAfee promptly began finding out how to meet the *Carpathia* when it arrived. Two more Park grads and old schoolmates of the Caldwells', Jack Carlisle and Luther Bicknell, came over from Princeton, New Jersey, where they were in McCormick Theological Seminary, also eager to meet their old friends.

But first the *Carpathia* had to retrace her route across the Atlantic and get back to New York. It was not a pleasant trip; in fact, it was "a slow, hazardous trip—it was stormy all the way to New York . . . but we were safe," Albert commented. Maybe Sylvia was seasick again during the storms on the cramped *Carpathia*, which probably rolled and pitched just as she had feared back in Naples. As fellow survivor Marie G. Young said, "The last few days of the voyage were taxing because rain kept the passengers crowded in the library, the wail of the foghorn sounding continually." The ship finally entered New York late at night on April 18. Albert was astonished by the reporters who lined the Hudson River, shouting questions in the pouring rain and the dark. As the *Carpathia* slid toward its dock, people lining the bank of the river kept calling, "How many were saved? How many were saved?" Albert reckoned he heard that question shouted fifty times from the bank. All throughout the *Carpathia*'s sad return voyage, people ashore telegraphed survivors, and the crew doled out the messages as the ship entered the harbor in New York. "And," Sylvia noted sadly, "as the names of some were called, they rushed eagerly forward, hoping, yes sure, that it was a message from their lost. I can see a woman now, as her name was called, press her hands together and raise her hands to heaven and say, 'My God' in a tone as tho she was giving thanks that her husband had been saved."

However, no other husbands had been saved. "It was but another disappointment," Sylvia grieved.

As they prepared to get off the *Carpathia*, "An amusing but pitiful incident," as Sylvia described it, served to illustrate how bedraggled the formerly prosperous middle-class Caldwells looked. "We all had tried to fix up as best we could. I had the little coat, made of the steamer rug on my baby and a dirty blanket over his head. Poor darling, he looked like a little Italian immigrant," Sylvia said. She had been given a few necessities, which she had tied up in a donated colorful shawl, "and with this in my hand, I looked as tho I might well be the mother of an Italian baby."

Sylvia recounted, "Two steamship inspectors came into the second cabin dining room [aboard the *Carpathia*], looked around, scowled and said, 'Is this steerage?'" Sylvia laughed halfheartedly. "I don't blame you for asking that," she said, realizing indeed how far she had fallen in terms of prosperity. This was a bad-tasting experience for Sylvia; in the eyes of most Americans of the era, Italians were undesirable immigrants. Having been middle-class tourists a few days before, the Caldwells truly had come down in the world.

No matter how bad they looked, they were grateful—*so* grateful—to be setting foot on American soil again.

But a possible menace was also waiting there on that blessed American soil. According to one estimate, 25,000 people were milling about the pier where the *Carpathia* was expected, hoping to catch a glimpse of the survivors. Three hundred policemen cordoned off the pier from the crowd. The oglers weren't the problem for the Caldwells, however; their would-be menace was, in fact, cleverly disguised as a mission of mercy. Thirty-five ambulances were waiting for the *Titanic*'s passengers as they disembarked. The ambulances had to force their way through the crowds by ringing gongs, and then the vehicles got to drive onto the cavernous dockhouse, a covered affair that had been cleared out to receive the *Titanic*'s passengers. The door was shut behind the ambulances. Because the mayor had ordered police to keep newsmen from communicating with passengers, an enterprising writer trolling for famous people to write about turned to the ambulances instead. He asked a pastor waiting with a private ambulance whom the ambulance was for. The pastor was the Presbyterian Reverend Dr. William Carter of the

Madison Avenue Reformed Church, who told the writer that the ambulance was reserved for Miss Sylvia Caldwell. "Who is she?" the writer must have asked. Carter replied that Sylvia "is known in church circles as a mission worker in foreign fields."

In reality, of course, Sylvia was hardly known by anyone as a "worker." Officials in the Foreign Missions Board office in New York mainly knew her as someone who had *not* worked in a year. Missionaries in Siam suspected her of skipping out on her duties and illicitly squirreling away money to come home before her contract was up. Carter's answer, therefore, seems a tad disingenuous. Could he have been sent with the ambulance to take Sylvia for the diagnosis R. C. Jones had advised?

Carter may have been doing just that. The *New York Herald* also ran a write-up of Carter's attempt to pick up Sylvia, revealing a no-nonsense purpose. The *Herald* reported, "The Rev. William D. Carter, pastor of the Madison Avenue Reformed Church, was at the pier with a private ambulance awaiting Miss Sylvia Caldwell, one of the survivors. She is one of the Church's foreign mission workers. Miss Caldwell will be taken directly to the Presbyterian Hospital."

To a casual reader of the *Herald*, this looked like an act of compassion, the church racing to the aid of one of its own. The casual reader would have nodded in sympathy. However, the casual reader had not seen R. C. Jones' recommendation that Sylvia be examined by church-appointed doctors before settling the Caldwells' account. The fact that in neither interview the pastor mentioned taking Albert and Alden along hinted that Sylvia was destined to go without the pleading young husband or the appealing young baby to intervene in a diagnosis, even though Albert and especially Alden might have needed medical attention after the dire circumstances on the open sea. For that reason it seems the ambulance may have been scheduled before the Caldwells had ever been caught in an open lifeboat mid-Atlantic. Likewise, Carter's identification of Sylvia as "Miss Sylvia Caldwell" made it sound as though she were not married; she would normally have gone by "Mrs. A. F. Caldwell." It does seem Albert was deliberately being excluded from Sylvia's medical exam.

Perhaps, then, it was fortunate for the Caldwells that there was someone else waiting for them inside the pier enclosure besides Carter and his ambulance. H. B. McAfee had been allowed into the Cunard Line's dockhouse to meet them as a "relative." He wasn't really related, but Park College had meant so much to them both that he might as well have been. He arrived at the dockhouse an hour before *Carpathia* reached her destination. "A crowd of more than three thousand persons were gathered at the dockhouse, whiling away time by inventing various rumors as reason for the ship's delay," he said. For one thing, the *Carpathia* stopped at the White Star Line pier to return the *Titanic*'s lifeboats—the only sad remainder of the ship. As McAfee told it, the rumor went around "that *Titanic*'s dead were being carried ashore in that manner." And then another rumor circulated, saying that a deadly strain of measles had broken out among the *Titanic* survivors on the *Carpathia*, "and the dead from this malady were being sent ashore. This was believed until the *Carpathia* moved to dock."

The gossip ceased as the *Carpathia* came into view. "The crowd held its breath in an agony of suspense," McAfee said. Some of the survivors had to be carried down. "Cries of recognition"—and surely relief—"heralded the appearance of each *Titanic* survivor on the gangway." McAfee was impressed with the "true chivalry and unselfishness of an American crowd" as the simultaneously joyful and sad disembarking began. "Each individual of the throng was desperately eager to meet his or her own relatives or friends," he said. "Yet when someone in a far away corner saw a friend in the gangway, the members of the crowd fell back and made wide lanes for the friends to meet each other as swiftly and with as little hindrance as possible. There was no hurry, no rush, no selfish surging toward the gangplank. Everyone seemed overjoyed that any other person should have found his beloved."

The survivors were assigned to gangways based on class, so McAfee was stationed near the second class gangplank. There were some horrible moments there. McAfee described one of them:

A lone woman left the ship and as she appeared on the [gangplank] her husband called, "Thank God, my wife is saved." As she approached within, he anxiously inquired about the two little ones with her. "They were lost," she told him. And that great strong man, with a cry that seared

every heart in the dockhouse, crumpled to the ground in a dead faint . . .
The men of that crowd wept as bitterly as did the women.

After awhile the Caldwells emerged—a family intact. The three clung
together, grateful to see McAfee—perhaps more grateful than McAfee
knew, as he provided cover from that waiting ambulance. McAfee took
them to a hotel, the Chelsea. By that kindness, Sylvia avoided Carter and
an examination that had possibly been ordered with a view to reclaiming
the family's expensive, expensive journey from Siam to America. Even if
the Caldwells had still had the $100 ($2,183 today) in gold, the money
would not have covered even the *Titanic* ticket ($2,919 today), much less
the voyage to Singapore, the passage through the Indian Ocean and the
Suez up to Naples, the train tickets and housing and food bills through
Europe to London. And Carter had no way of knowing that they had not
taken their savings with them off the *Titanic*. The now penniless Caldwells
would have needed years to pay off the bill for the trip.

But perhaps Carter was not there to expose Sylvia as a fraud or a hy-
pochondriac. Perhaps the ambulance was sent on a true mercy trip to help
a sick missionary recover; indeed, Carter was known as a crusader against
pastor burnout, and tending to Sylvia could have been part of his crusade.
In fact, as Albert recalled it when he was well into his eighties, "Of course
the missionary society met us there and took us to a hotel." Perhaps H. B.
McAfee had been sent by the Board of Foreign Missions to collect the
Caldwells and get them to a hotel, and no one bothered to tell Carter of
the duplicate effort. Or perhaps Carter was deliberately standing by to aid
McAfee, should Sylvia be very ill. The *Carpathia* did make land at night;
perhaps Sylvia did not deliberately avoid Carter but simply missed him in
the dark. As McAfee reported, there were 3,000 people waiting in the enclosed area; it would have been easy for any two of them to miss each other.

Any of those scenarios could well be true. However, the circumstances at
least made it *appear* that the Board of Foreign Missions had indeed heeded
Jones's suggestion, as chairman of the Siam mission's Executive Committee,
that Sylvia be scrutinized. Having followed the Conybeare saga, having been
condemned for saving their travel money, having seen Sylvia's diagnosis voted

down by five fellow missionaries (including the chairman), the Caldwells might well have known or guessed that they were under surveillance, and they gratefully fell into McAfee's unsuspecting arms. Or perhaps McAfee, a loyal Park College friend tipped off by his brother Cleland, was protecting Sylvia from an examination designed to ensnare them.

It was probably a good thing that Sylvia was not whisked off to be examined the minute she returned, because she was so relieved that she appeared momentarily to be OK. Joseph E. McAfee, brother to H. B. and Cleland, lived in Brooklyn. He wrote to their brother Lowell, who had long ago recommended Albert for the job in Siam, "I have never known this city to lie under such a pall as that caused by what one of the papers called 'The *Titanic* Tragedy'. The *Carpathia* docked last night, and the adjacent streets were a sight to behold. The Caldwells were able to go directly to a hotel. All seemed in good health and remarkable spirits considering their terrible experience." But shortly the trauma of the voyage or the lingering tropical malady overwhelmed Sylvia. Joseph E. told Lowell,

> Mrs. Caldwell is reported ill today, has been under a physician's care and has seen very few persons. The baby is apparently in very good health . . . We think and speak of little else than the tragedy between items of routine business. Politics and baseball are apparently forgotten by the whole population, and the newspapers have scarcely anything to say of them or anything else except the disaster.

Thus, Sylvia finally did go under a doctor's care in New York, and even if the physician was charged with second-guessing Walker's diagnosis back in Siam, the trauma of the *Titanic* had wiped out much of the logic behind a second diagnosis such as Jones had advocated. Sylvia by now could have been suffering from neurasthenia or nerves or shock or the effects of the dire cold or the effects of prolonged seasickness. The ordeal of the escape around the world had taken its toll, and it would have been a surprise if she *weren't* exhibiting symptoms of some sort.

And indeed, the church would have made deep trouble for itself by pursuing *Titanic* victims and money that had gone down with the ship. Such a story, had it gotten out, would have made the church look thoughtless at best, demonic at worst. The only answer was to let the matter drop. The Caldwells' debt, such as it was, had been wiped clean. The sinking of the *Titanic* had effectively nullified any claims of the Foreign Missions Board against the Caldwells.

It all came out even. The Caldwells' savings, which had cast so much suspicion on them, had gone to the bottom of the Atlantic. If their debt was cancelled, so were their tainted gains.

WHEN THEY ARRIVED IN New York, Albert, Sylvia, and Alden had nothing but the rumpled clothes on their backs. After two and a half years of ministering to the poor and spiritually lost, the Caldwells were poor and perhaps feeling spiritually lost themselves. However, friends and strangers pitched in to furnish them with material things. Mrs. Wallace Radcliffe, a church worker in Washington, D.C., pleaded to Presbyterian women in her area to donate to the Caldwells, and she would see that the money got to the family in New York. A Washington newspaper joined in the appeal by noting, "When the *Titanic* sank Mrs. Caldwell lost all of her baggage and money, and when the *Carpathia* docked the couple were penniless."

That appeal and other efforts on the Caldwells' behalf relieved their situation momentarily. "The best of every thing was provided for us," Sylvia said. "We were all clad in new and pretty clothing. My baby who only had a nightie and a coat made out of steamer rug, was given a complete outfit." A women's missionary magazine commented, "Loving hands provided for their every need when they reached New York." Albert had hastened to telegraph to his parents that they were home and alive, and no doubt their families were gratefully gearing up to do all they could to help.

Another person Albert contacted was Sam Conybeare, who had written a letter to the Caldwells, perhaps addressed to them in New York after the Conybeares heard about the shipwreck. In replying, Albert found out that entrepreneurs worked fast in New York; someone had already printed up a postcard depicting an artist's rendering of the *Titanic* cutting through the waters of the Atlantic, perilously close to an iceberg. "OCEAN LINER TITANIC—LARGEST STEAMER IN THE WORLD," the front of the postcard read.

"Sunk by iceberg on maiden trip off Halifax, April 15, 1912; 1,500 people drowned. Length, 882 feet; breadth, 92 feet; number of steel decks, 11; watertight bulkeads, 15; passengers accommodated, 2,500; crew, 860; tonnage registered, 45,000; tonnage displacement, 66,000; cost, $7,500,000."

Albert got one of the souvenir cards, flipped it over, and wrote on the back to Conybeare, "Rec'd your good letter. Leave for home tomorrow morning. Have lots to tell later. People are treating us lovely here. Had an awful experience but we are very thankful. Albert." He dropped it in the mail on April 21, less than a week after the *Titanic* sank. Indeed, the postcard artist had worked fast to cash in on the wreck.

The postcard, which made the disaster into a souvenir, indicated a darkly commercial side of American fascination with the shipwreck. However, mostly the *Titanic*'s survivors found that Americans were sympathetic and generous. A rich New York doctor stepped in to take care of the Caldwells' shipboard dining companions, Lottie Collyer and little Madge. Unlike Sylvia, Lottie was conflicted about being saved. "Oh mother," she wrote Harvey's mother, "how can I live without him. I wish I'd gone with him if they had not wrenched Madge from me I should have stayed and gone with him. But they threw her into the boat and pulled me in too but she was so calm and I know he would rather I lived for her sake otherwise she would have been an orphan." She reported to her in-laws that their host doctor had collected a good deal of money for them and "loaded us with clothes," and a man was soon going to take her to pick up money from the funds being donated by the public.

Indeed, much was donated. The Chelsea did not charge the Caldwells for their room. Eventually, the railroad out to Illinois would give them a ticket for free. "I am sure no survivor now, is penniless," Sylvia said gratefully a few weeks later.

Even the missioned-to back in Siam—or, rather, in Siam's northern province of Laos—were forced to sacrifice for the well-being of the *Titanic* survivors. On April 19, Dr. Arthur Judson Brown, secretary of the Board of Foreign Missions, wrote to the Laos mission that the Board would not be able to provide funds to relieve malaria that was plaguing Laos. He said, "All our relief funds are now exhausted and the public appeals that are being made for the relief of the survivors and dependent relatives in connection with the steamship *Titanic* now sweeps all public interest in that direction." To increase the sympathy factor, he went on, "The Rev. and Mrs. A. F. Caldwell and their baby, returning from Siam, were among the passengers on that ill-fated steamer but we are rejoiced to know that they were among the saved."

The Reverend and Mrs. Caldwell—although "Reverend" was not actually his title—were as eager as everyone else was to learn all the details of the *Titanic*. Very soon after the wreck, they bought a copy of the Memorial Edition of *Story of the Wreck of the Titanic*. Not only did it provide a wide array of firsthand accounts, but it also featured a special introduction by the Reverend Henry Van Dyke, a well-known Presbyterian minister. The book was edited by Marshall Everett, who was billed as "The Great Descriptive Writer." The volume, published almost immediately after the *Titanic* sank, was produced so hastily that the text was bound upside down in relation to the cover in the Caldwells' copy. It gave an account of the Collyers, a fact which very much appealed to Sylvia. What was truly exciting, however, was that it mentioned Alden, if somewhat obliquely. The Caldwells' copy was no doubt meant to be a treasure for him someday. It quoted Lawrence Beesley, who had shared the Caldwells' lifeboat: "As the boat began to descend two ladies were pushed hurriedly through the crowd on B deck and heaved over into the boat, and a baby of 10 months passed down after them." In his own book shortly thereafter, Beesley described two ladies, followed by the three Caldwells, including 10-month-old Alden. If Albert minded the mistake as to his gender in the *Story of the Wreck of the Titanic*, he didn't say. It is likely that Everett, in his haste to produce the book, simply misquoted Beesley's story. However, if Beesley really did at first recall Albert as female, it might have been a natural mistake in all the confusion and hubbub, as Albert was carrying the baby. Everyone seemed to remember that.

The volume also featured a speech by William Jennings Bryan, whom Albert had met in 1908 when Bryan, then running for president, had arrived at Park College unexpectedly between campaign stops and had spoken extemporaneously. He had missed a train connection in Kansas City, and rather than waste time at the station, he decided to visit the college.

OCEAN LINER TITANIC—LARGEST STEAMER IN THE WORLD.

Sunk by iceberg on maiden trip off Halifax, April 15, 1912; 1,500 people drowned. Length, 882 feet; breadth, 92 feet; number of steel decks, 11; watertight bulkheads, 15; passengers accommodated, 2,500; crew, 860; tonnage registered, 45,000; tonnage displacement, 66,000; cost, $7,500,000.

*Entrepreneurs leaped into action to sell items related to the* Titanic *disaster. Albert acquired this card in New York and mailed it less than a week after the disaster. By the time Albert sent this postcard to Sam Conybeare, the Caldwells were looking forward to going home the next day.*

This Space For Writing Messages.

Sunday morning
Rec'd your good
letter. I leave for
home tomorrow
morning. Have
lots to tell. Later.
People are treating
us lovely here.
I had an awful
experience but
are very thankful
Albert

NEW YORK, N.Y. STA.
APR 21
3 PM
1912

Prof. S. E. Conybeare
Cedar Rapids High School
Cedar Rapids
Ia.

This side for the Address only.

He telegraphed ahead, and the whole town, it seemed, turned out to hear him. The Park College Democratic Club, of which Albert was a member, had their picture taken with the great man. Now Bryan and the Caldwells shared the aftermath of the *Titanic* tragedy as well. Bryan spoke about the *Titanic* at an event billed as a "memorial meeting" on Sunday, April 21, at the Broadway Theater in New York City, and perhaps Albert attended while Sylvia recovered. The theater was reportedly "jammed . . . from orchestra to topmost balcony." Bryan called for reform in the transAtlantic passenger service, and his speech was preserved in the Caldwells' copy of the book:

> I venture the prediction that the wireless system will be made more immediately effective and efficient over a wider area and that the chance of danger will be diminished. I venture the assertion . . . that better preparations will be made with the lifeboats for the safety of passengers. I venture the assertion that less attention will be paid to comforts and luxuries that can be dispensed with and more thought given to the lives of those entrusted to the care of those shipbuilders and shipowners. I venture to assert also that the mania for speed will receive a check and that people will not be so anxious to get across the ocean in *the shortest time* as they will be to *get across*." [Emphasis added.]

Bryan offered some good suggestions, and surely Sylvia and Albert seconded them.

Although the Caldwells were given all they could use and had lots of friends in New York who were caring for them, Sylvia reportedly lapsed into nervous shock soon after the *Carpathia* arrived. She had been under a doctor's care, but the true cure was obvious: she needed to go home. She needed that rest cure that her doctors in Siam had prescribed so long ago.

# 8

# TOSSED ON THE OCEAN OF LIFE

As the Caldwells boarded a train from New York heading westward toward Albert's parents' home in Illinois, it was pretty clear how blessed they were. True, they had lost everything: Alden's official birth records, their Parisian clothes, their London woolens, their camera, souvenirs, a substantial sum in gold pieces, all their household goods, everything they had accumulated in their marriage except for what they wore off the *Titanic* or were donated afterward. They had even lost their jobs. But they had each other—and parents, siblings, and friends. They also seemed to have dodged the issue of payment for the passage home from Siam.

Had the *Titanic* arrived in New York as originally scheduled, Sylvia would have gone on to Washington to speak to Presbyterian churchwomen about the Jane Hays Memorial Fund to build a school in Bangkok. That would just have to wait, she told them. She didn't bother informing the ladies there, who had been collecting money on the Caldwells' behalf, that she and Albert had resigned (under some suspicion) and would not be going back to Siam. The church ladies believed, according to the *Washington Post,* that the Caldwells were only home on furlough. Instead the Caldwells headed home on the Pennsylvania Railroad, taking train No. 15 on the New York-to-Chicago route. Everyone aboard knew they were *Titanic* survivors and kept congratulating them. They had a joyous stop in Pittsburgh, celebrating briefly there with Sylvia's family. Chambers Harbaugh, Sylvia's father, was visiting in Glenshaw from Colorado Springs. She found him waiting on the platform at Union Station in Pittsburgh to see his daughter and son-in-law and meet his grandson for the first time. Sylvia's cousin, Mrs. F. K. Head, came, too.

As a former Glenshaw girl, Sylvia starred in the *Pittsburg Daily Dispatch's* account of their triumphant reunion. "Mrs. Caldwell showed no nervousness in telling of her experiences of a biting cold night on a rocking lifeboat with her 10-months-old baby, clothed in little else than a steamer rug. 'The baby never even cried,' she said with a smile." Indeed, Alden showed the same good behavior in Pittsburgh. The travelers had an hour's layover in town, and the baby "slept in its berth in the Pullman, one hand outstretched and a smile on its face. Passengers tiptoed up and looked at the baby."

The Caldwells' train chugged onward to Illinois, where Albert's parents would greet them. On the Burlington train No. 11 on April 23, when the train stopped in Monmouth, Illinois, a newspaper reporter asked if they could be interviewed. They "submitted readily and cheerfully" to the reporter's questions, although Albert did most of the talking.

As had been reported in Pittsburgh, everyone on the train had found out the Caldwells were *Titanic* survivors. They were celebrities, and Alden was chief among them, credited already by his parents with saving his father's life. As the news report ran:

> The family naturally was glad to be nearing their journey's end, and was the object of interest to many of their fellow passengers as the train drew near Monmouth. The baby especially came in for his share of attention and was hailed as the hero who saved his father's life. He had not suffered from the exposure and his rosy cheeks indicated good health.

Alden was the hero, but they all knew they owed God the biggest debt of thanks when they finally arrived home to Biggsville. A couple of weeks after the three *Titanic* survivors arrived at William and Fannie's house, the Reverend Caldwell at last baptized little Alden, now eleven months old. They had his picture made, both formally and informally, in honor of the baptism. The ceremony marked an even greater spiritual meaning beyond launching Alden into the church. It reflected deep reverence and gratitude to God for the rescue of Alden and his parents. Albert was convinced that his father's prayers on April 14 had directed the stoker to hail them, and with such divine intervention, something bigger must be afoot. But what was it? As one newspaper commented about Albert, "Since he is saved, the Lord must have something for him to do."

INDEED, WHAT WERE THEY to do? Penniless and jobless, they had to do *something*. Albert started by filing official documents requesting aid to cover their property that went down with the *Titanic*. He filed an insurance claim for $1,411 in lost goods. On a different document collected by the Red Cross, he listed the property they had lost: the $100 in cash, as well as their clothing, silverware, table linen, and household effects, all of which he valued at $1,300 ($28,432 today), far greater than the $400 ($9,737 today) that the Board of Foreign Missions had granted them to furnish their home in Bangkok. Albert had worried that $400 would not be enough, and no doubt they had added to their furnishings from their own salaries; also, they had brought over wedding gifts, which had also been lost. Perhaps the Red Cross claim also included compensation for suffering; the Red Cross noted, "Both parents suffered severely from shock." Red Cross records even characterized Sylvia as an invalid. Perhaps the Caldwells spiced up the details of their suffering a little—or a lot. Perhaps they were still worried about being charged by the church for their travel home, and they were rebuilding the nest egg for that purpose. The Red Cross did note that they got $1,000 from funds collected to aid *Titanic* victims, which the Caldwells used to furnish their home.

But insurance money and emergency assistance were not the same as a salary, and there was that nagging fact that they had lost their jobs. They needed an income. Their first instinct was to relate their experiences on the ship. Albert went on the Chautauqua and lecture circuit, first speaking at Park College less than a month after the tragedy. Sylvia did not attend the Park speech, which was a surprise to her old schoolmate Addie B. Wyeth. Addie, who didn't like Sylvia, was not eager to hear Sylvia's *Titanic* story, which she was sure would be overblown. Addie wrote to a friend, "The Caldwells will be here from the *Titanic* wreck for Sunday [for a chapel talk]. I am wondering if I could escape to the city. I hate a palaver and a slobber and I'll wager my next salary that Sylvia Harbaugh can put up the tears and the nerves." Clearly Sylvia had been expected to speak, and as a noted declaimer and actress in her college days, she would have told the story well and with dramatic flair. Instead of commanding tears and nerves, however, Sylvia was still recovering from nervous shock, according to Albert.

Of course, given the ugly doubts about her illness, if she were now well she may have stayed out of sight on purpose. Had she spoken as Addie had expected, Sylvia would have been surrounded by hundreds of Presbyterian witnesses who could attest to her health.

For whatever reason, Albert spoke by himself at Park, where he "gave a very interesting account . . . before a very large audience in the chapel," according to the student newspaper. In May the Caldwells visited Colorado Springs, the home of Sylvia's parents, and Albert spoke at First Presbyterian Church. Again, Sylvia did not speak, although she would have been the natural choice as one of Colorado's prettiest girls (as the *Washington Post* had called her) and as an accomplished actress/speaker. Perhaps she was still ill, although she was able to give a vivid account of the *Titanic* to the local newspaper. Maybe she was deliberately keeping a low profile in front of Presbyterian audiences. She did, however, eventually speak to her father-in-law's Presbyterian church in Biggsville. Albert went on to spend a season "on the Chautauqua and lecture platform," as he described it, collecting pay in return for his speeches about the *Titanic* and racking up good press coverage. At the Chautauqua in Oregon, Missouri, Albert even got to speak the day after his hero, William Jennings Bryan.

Sylvia wrote a short booklet, *Women of the Titanic Disaster*. The horrible experiences on the *Titanic* did not dim her missionary's zeal for God. She dedicated the booklet by borrowing the dedication from *Story of the Wreck of the Titanic:* "To those who by their deeds and acts followed in the footsteps of Him who suffered on the Cross, and who now sleep in unmarked graves of the sea." She quoted Henry Ward Beecher, again in a passage lifted straight from *Story of the Wreck of the Titanic:*

> Oh, what a burial was here! Not as when one is bourne from his home among weeping throngs and gently carried to the green fields . . . It was an ocean grave . . . Down, down they sank, and the quick returning waters smoothed out every ripple and left the sea as though it had not been!

Clearly, *Story of the Wreck of the Titanic* had impressed Sylvia. The primary inspiration for her own *Women of the Titanic Disaster,* however, came from

*Pictured here are Fannie Gates Caldwell, Albert Francis Caldwell, old Francis Gates, and Alden Gates Caldwell in a four-generations picture made shortly after the* Titanic. *In an unusual twist, it was the bottom two generations who nearly did not survive long enough to make the picture.*

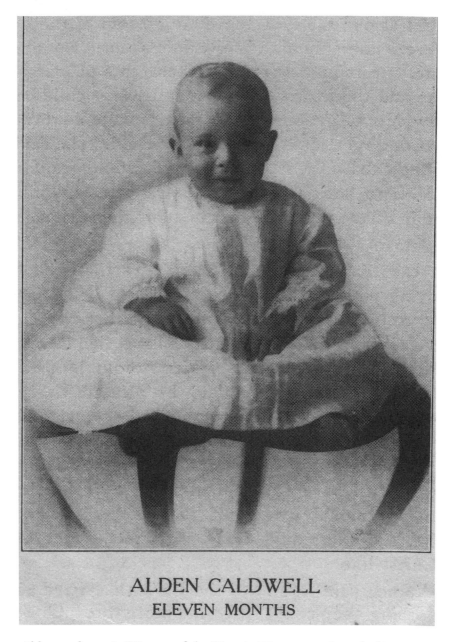

## ALDEN CALDWELL
### ELEVEN MONTHS

*Alden as shown in* Women of the Titanic Disaster, *written by his mother. This formal portrait was probably the one taken on the occasion of his baptism in May 1912.*

Alden. She wrote, "I have been sitting in the dusk, rocking to sleep the precious young life that was spared to me from the last great disaster and my heart goes out to the heart broken mothers whose babes have been snatched from their arms." The screams of the foreign woman crying for her baby still rang in her ears. "Babes?" she went on. "Yes and husbands, breadwinners for the little ones. It brings tears to eyes of you, who can comprehend in a tiny degree the sorrow and suffering of the broken circles."

She protested that she was not a writer, but she picked up her pen anyway. Mainly she wanted to praise the women of the *Titanic* for their "fortitude and bravery." It was also a chance to stand up for women who had outlived their husbands in the disaster, and the even smaller number of women, like herself, whose husbands had made it safely off the ship. She spoke reverently of Lottie Collyer's plans to continue westward to do what her husband had intended to do—to work to support little Madge, or "little Margorie, as we called her," Sylvia said, misspelling the child's name but also indicating that their brief shipboard friendship had revolved around their children. "I call that heroism," Sylvia wrote. "Yes, greater than that of the wife dying with her husband. She saved herself and was willing to live and suffer for the sake of her child." Slipping into the romantic notions of the day, Sylvia commented, "How much easier it would have been to have died in his arms." That comment certainly indicated how difficult it would be for the widowed Mrs. Collyer and so many like her to make a new life without a husband. Sylvia quoted Mrs. Collyer, probably from the newspaper (there is no evidence they ever met again), "I cannot think of life without him but if he could speak, I know he would be pleased to know I stayed with Margorie." Sylvia's heart went out to Lottie and the other widowed women, who were so vulnerable in a foreign country. Sylvia herself had a college education and career experience overseas and a husband. So many of the *Titanic*'s women did not have those advantages.

As Sylvia described Lottie Collyer, "I was proud to welcome such a heroine to my country. This bereaved woman would go about comforting others and then come back saying, 'How much I have to be thankful for. I feel it when I see so many, worse off than I.'" Sylvia admired Lottie's Christlike trait of thinking of others, even in her time of great sorrow. Sylvia followed the story of Madge and Lottie in the newspapers and was pleased to see they were offered a home in California.

All in all, Sylvia was amazed about what women had done as they stumbled off the *Carpathia*, widowed and penniless, homeless and supposedly helpless. "I have never seen such self-possessed women. I have never seen such unselfishness among women. I have never seen such bravery among women," she wrote. "You, oh sorrowing women of the disaster, have caused the name of women to be raised to a higher pedestal." Nor did she forget the women of the *Carpathia* and of America, who had stepped in even on her behalf with care and donations for her family—and she had her husband still. Sylvia wrote, "You, oh ministering women, who have so bountifully and tenderly cared for the suffering, I say may God in his richest fullness bless you."

She concluded with Hall Caine's hymn for the survivors of the *Titanic*, noting that it was sung to the tune of "God, Our Help in Ages Past." Prayers had been said for the dead, but in using that hymn, Sylvia prayed for the living, the survivors who had to go on. Thus, she prayed not just for the *Titanic*'s women; she also prayed for her husband.

ALBERT HAD TO FIND his way in the world all over again. His career in Siam gone, his earnings from that job gone, his material gains all gone, he had to find something permanent to do. Curiously, two different sources of the era assumed he went into the ministry, and they were sources who should have known. One was the Presbyterian Board of Foreign Missions' Secretary Dr. Arthur Judson Brown, who called him the Reverend A. F. Caldwell in some official missionary business. The other was a newspaper reporter in Roseville, Illinois, who published an extensive interview with Albert just a week and a half after the *Titanic* sank. By then Albert and Sylvia were at home in Biggsville with Albert's parents, not far from Roseville. The article clearly called Albert the Reverend Caldwell. In truth, Albert was never actually ordained as a minister, but it appears he was given the honorary title as a result of the *Titanic* disaster.

Albert had no such title, but it was clear he was anxiously backpedaling over the events of his life and considering where he stood with God as

## HYMN FOR SURVIVORS OF THE TITANIC
### By Hall Caine
#### To the tune of "God, Our Help in Ages Past."

Lord of the everlasting hills,
  God of the boundless sea,
Help us through all the shocks of fate
  To keep our trust in Thee.

When nature's unrelenting arm
  Sweep us like withes away,
Maker of man, be Thou our strength
  And our eternal stay.

When blind, insensate, heartless force
  Puts out our passing breath,
Make us to see Thy guiding light,
  In darkness and in death.

Beneath the roll of soundless waves
  Our best and bravest lie;
Give us to feel their spirits live
  Immortal in the sky.

We are Thy children, frail and small,
  Formed of the lowly sod,
Comfort our bruised and bleeding souls,
  Father and Lord and God.

*A page from Sylvia's 1912 booklet,* Women of the Titanic Disaster, *shows the "Hymn for Survivors of the* Titanic*" and a contemporary artist's depiction of the shipwreck.*

he tried to put his family's lives back on track. Left with nothing after the disaster except, gratefully, his wife and baby to support, Albert thought briefly of an almost unbelievable career path, one that probably illustrated his desperation or perhaps indeed mirrored a lingering desire to become a minister. Incredibly, he considered going back to Siam. Possibly he was thinking of signs from God. Their Siamese salary that they had saved under less-than-aboveboard conditions, the money that was supposed to help launch them back into America, was now entombed two miles down in the tragic remains of the *Titanic*, along with household goods they had acquired for and used in Siam. Maybe it was a symbol from heaven. Albert wrote to his old boss W. G. McClure in Bangkok that "they might be ready to return to Siam after a while," as McClure reported in a letter to Arthur Brown of the Foreign Missions Board, adding, "He says that they were providentially saved from the wreck of the '*Titanic*' for a purpose, and it is their wish to find out that purpose and to do it." McClure was a little wistful about Albert's letter. "I believe that he at least, would be glad to return, and I think he would make a fine missionary, especially after the experiences they had after leaving Siam," McClure said. Someone who received McClure's letter in New York underlined the statement that Albert would make a fine missionary, but wrote in the margin at that point, "Ask if Miss[ion] Ex[ecutive] Com[mittee] wants," although the scrawl was ambiguous enough to have perhaps read, "Ask if Mrs. Ex Com wants. Perhaps the double meaning was intended.

It was clear from Albert's letter to McClure that the *Titanic* experience had shaken his faith in his own wisdom. And the letter offered a broad hint that Sylvia was feeling much better now. Almost certainly, however, Albert had not asked her about going back to Siam before he wrote to McClure. One can hardly imagine her agreeing to such a thing, although Albert made it sound like she did. Family stories later that Sylvia absolutely put her foot down about Siam probably stemmed from this period.

Faced with the need to start a new career, Albert turned not to the religious side of his missionary duties, but to the teaching side. He had taught school in Siam, and that was the career he would follow now. In 1912 he became principal of Aledo High School in Aledo, Illinois. It was a happy time. A family photo taken about a year after the *Titanic* shows the three of them as the picture of health, Sylvia fully recovered from any illness or anxiety about their future. Alden, now sturdy and active, held a ball in the picture, while Albert held on to him. It was a picture of a family whose world had righted itself. They were back in America, away from the tropics that had sapped their will to serve God as they had planned, safely back home after the *Titanic*, and Albert had a permanent job.

They got an odd thing in the mail some time during that first year back

*Albert as the youthful principal of Aledo (Illinois) High School, 1912.*

in the United States: the photo of them that their London friend had taken on the deck of the *Titanic*. It was a terrible picture; none of their faces really showed clearly, with Sylvia bending over and Alden slumped like a lump in his Daddy's arms. It was an awful likeness. But of course it was a rare thing, a treasure, a photo from the *Titanic*. All throughout their childhood, Alden and his little brother Raymond Milton Caldwell, born December 21, 1914, would trot out the picture when they wanted to impress their friends.

In Aledo Albert served as principal, taught five classes each day, coached the basketball team, directed the male glee club, and taught Sunday School. He himself sang in the Sunday School chorus and in the church choir. He was as busy as he ever had been in Siam. He liked his work as an educator, but if he wanted to make education a permanent career in a bigger town, be probably needed further schooling. Thus, after two years he moved his family to Ames, Iowa, so he could do post-graduate work at Iowa State College, and so he could take over as principal of the much bigger Ames High School.

Best of all, Sam and Bess Conybeare were there! The couples had remained close. Bess had come from their home in Cedar Rapids, Iowa, to visit the Caldwells in Biggsville in July 1912, shortly after the *Titanic*. Now the Conybeares lived in Ames, too, and Sam was teaching journalism at Iowa State. Conybeare was still plying the business side of things, teaching advertising. It was truly cutting-edge work, as journalism was a brand new course of college study anywhere in the United States in 1914. For the Caldwells and the Conybeares, their renewed friendship in Iowa was an opportunity to celebrate their blessings. They had all escaped Siam, and the Caldwells had survived the *Titanic*. Life had been renewed afresh for both families. They were all survivors.

Albert won the respect of his pupils at Ames High School; they dedicated the 1916 edition of their yearbook, the *Spirit*, to him "In appreciation of his faithful and successful efforts to promote the welfare of Ames High." After his two-year stint as principal, Albert sold cars for the Overland Motor Company for two years. Then he was back in education with a bigger title: he became superintendent of schools in Richland Center, Wisconsin. He ran a four-year high school there that in 1920 sported eleven teachers and

*The Caldwells' world had righted itself a year after the* Titanic, *as was clear in this happy photograph.*

*Alden and little brother Raymond Milton Caldwell play in a wagon, circa*
*spring 1917. Raymond was born late in 1914.*

264 students. The Caldwells loved Wisconsin, where they bought a home
on a lake that their family would return to for years and years.

But this term as an educator didn't last, either. Albert had discovered
while selling cars that he was a good salesman. In 1923, Albert left education for the last time and moved to Bloomington, Illinois, where he sold
life insurance with both Prudential Life and Massachusetts Life in 1924. He
switched companies, landing at State Farm Insurance in 1929. Outgoing
and chatty, he no doubt made a good insurance agent. He also became a
leader in the Bloomington community, heading the Bloomington Kiwanis
Club as its president in 1927.

ALBERT'S CAREER HAD BEEN chaotic, but things had already gotten more
tangled along career lines in the Caldwell household. Maybe because Albert
had had such a hard time settling on a career, or maybe because teenage
Alden would soon enough be college age and bills loomed, or maybe because she had been to college and was prepared to have a career, or maybe

because she just wanted to do it, Sylvia went to work. She got a job with State Farm Mutual Insurance on September 20, 1925, after they moved to Bloomington. The company was a new one and in need of smart, local workers; in fact, she was the eleventh person hired by the company on its route to becoming a colossus in the insurance industry. She was a policy underwriter at first. As a company newsletter described her work, "During the first few years in handling general office work, supervision of office records, etc., Mrs. Caldwell had the opportunity of acquiring complete first-hand knowledge of every phase of the company's affairs." This fact plus her education, the newsletter pointed out, made her invaluable to the president and founder of the company, G. J. Mecherle. In 1927, Sylvia became the secretary to Mecherle, who was, as she and Albert were, Presbyterian. Perhaps the Caldwells first met Mecherle at church.

Mecherle himself was a fascinating self-made man. His German father had come to America in 1852, setting up a farm in Merna, Illinois, before meeting and marrying his Quaker mother. George Jacob was their fifth child, born in 1877. He went to high school at his mother's insistence but only stayed a year, his leaving made painless when the Illinois governor closed the high school, which the governor thought was improperly housed at a local university. George slipped easily from student to farmer when his uncle offered him a tract of land on a rent-to-own basis. When George proved successful at farming, he married his neighbor, Mae Perry, in 1900. George was an excellent farmer but also a glib talker who had a gift for making others catch his vision of things, a talent enhanced by his excellence as a storyteller. He served as a county road commissioner just as automobiles were becoming popular. He thought a lot about automobiles and how they related to the farm.

Unfortunately, Mae developed a painful case of arthritis. Seventeen years after they married, the Mecherles rented out their prosperous farm in Illinois and moved to Florida, supposing that the moist heat of Florida would improve Mae's condition. It did not. George had thought he might sell real estate in Florida, but they moved back to Illinois, choosing to live in Bloomington specifically to be near a hospital for Mae's sake. Having considered a sales career in Florida, George now went into the insurance business in Bloomington, selling automobile insurance for the Union Automobile Indemnity Association. He bounced from there into another job selling tractors but kept thinking about insurance. Farmers often complained to him that they simply couldn't afford it—at least, not on their cars. George was frustrated for them. As the State Farm website puts it today, "Mecherle knew farmers drove less and had fewer accidents than city folk. He thought they should pay less for automobile insurance." Ultimately that knowledge of farmers and their needs, coupled with his desire to get into the insurance industry, blossomed into G. J. Mecherle's own business, which he named State Farm Mutual Automobile Insurance Company. His company would charge lower rates for farmers. In fact, Mecherle eventually pioneered insurance discounts for good drivers. He launched State Farm in 1922, and by 1927, he had opened his first branch office in California. State Farm was set to become the giant it is today.

As G. J. Mecherle's star was rising, however, stars seemed to be smashing to the ground in the Caldwell family. Albert traveled a lot for his work and was often away from home, and by now his marriage to Sylvia was in serious trouble.

Albert had had to relive the Clown's nightmarish lines from *The Winter's Tale* by witnessing the *Titanic* sink; now Sylvia was caught in her own nightmare scene reflecting her *Winter's Tale* role as Hermione, who had been accused of infidelity. There were rumors that Sylvia and Mr. Mecherle had developed an overly close friendship, the kind of rumor that wags from tongues the world over when it comes to bosses and secretaries. This one was fed by the fact that Mae Mecherle was an invalid. There is no evidence that Sylvia had any improper friendship with Mr. Mecherle; it could likely have just been vicious gossip. In fact, at one point, G. J. Mecherle saw some graffiti scrawled on the sidewalk outside the building, suggesting that company men were having romantic liaisons with company women. He called a meeting of all male employees, and, nearly in tears, told them such dalliances were not acceptable.

If such gossip had been directed at Sylvia, it was fueled mightily by Albert and Sylvia divorcing in 1930. Alden was nineteen and Raymond was sixteen. The marriage, which had started way too fast with a six-week trip across the Pacific, which had survived the desperate flight from Siam and the tragic voyage of the *Titanic*, and which had once seemed so blessed, had only lasted twenty-one years. The exact reason for the divorce is not known. Divorce was stylish in that era, but it was still a disappointing end to the college romance. Perhaps in the final analysis, Albert and Sylvia had simply married too young and moved around the world too fast and had not followed the career they had planned. In ironic ways, the *Titanic* seemed to have been the high-water mark of their marriage, the end of the idealistic youthful career they had chosen with such exuberance—in a place Albert liked and Sylvia did not—the last time all their plans were exactly aligned. True, they had been happy after that. But their marriage seemed to have foundered in the snarls of their later careers.

Awkwardly, Albert and Sylvia both still worked at State Farm. In 1933, though, Albert was transferred to the Richmond, Virginia, office, a promotion to the post of district agent. To some gossips, of course, it looked like a convenient relocation of an ex-husband. Albert was a successful agent for State Farm, although his office stationery mockingly reminded him at the bottom of the page, "Home Office, Bloomington, Illinois."

# 9

# NAVIGATING NEW WATERS

When Albert arrived in Richmond in 1933, he was no longer the good-looking fellow with a shock of light hair and a twinkling smile. By now he had lost his hair. He had had a mild stroke, and his mouth twisted ever so slightly. He still sported a good sense of humor and that old missionary zest for living, however. In Richmond, ever the charmer, he met a Southern girl. He was smitten. Jennie Congleton, the cute gal with the honeyed accent who had caught Albert's eye, was thrilled to catch his as well. Jennie was fifteen years younger than Albert, but she was well into her 30s—an old maid by local standards. Jennie had not had an easy life, although her mother, Jennie Whitley, had aspired to better. Hailing from Pantego in eastern North Carolina, Jennie Whitley had attended Staunton Female Academy in Staunton, Virginia, graduating in 1885. Certainly her parents had means and ambition for their daughter to send her to board so far from home. Jennie Whitley loved school. She took diligent class notes in appropriate parts of her Latin book, but on the endpapers of the textbook she doodled pictures and wrote of her friend Ida, "Ida and Ned Cameron will make a lovely couple." To this Ida responded by grabbing the book and writing that somebody—his name began with J—"and Jennie Whitley are <u>mashed</u> on each other." We don't know who that somebody was, because Jennie erased his name and crossed it out. Nevertheless, she saved a lock of hair in the book, possibly that of her crush. She also kept multiple essays that she composed. In one entitled "Education," she wrote:

> Education is the wheel upon which fortune turns. Men have started out in the world without a dollar in their pockets, and have slowly but firmly risen to eminence. How: I ask. By means of a good education. Of

all the blessings which it has pleased Providence to allow us to cultivate, there is not one which breathes a purer fragrance or bears a heavenlier aspect, than education.

Well-educated Jennie was interested in well-educated men, and she met one back in North Carolina, perhaps while she was teaching at Richland Academy. He was Asa Biggs Congleton, known in more alphabetical fashion

*Albert after he had moved to Richmond.*

as "A. B." During his examinations to qualify as a teacher in 1881, A. B. scored 90 or 95 for every subject except Geography (he got an 80 in that) and was given a First Grade certificate, the highest designation. He studied hard and pulled his Geography grade up to a 95 in 1883. However, A. B. was not able to make a living as a teacher. After he and Jennie Whitley married, their focus on education became a distant memory. The Congletons for generations had owned a family farm near Stokes, North Carolina, and A. B. went into farming. Jennie was frequently pregnant and frequently giving birth. First came Jim, then Edwin, then Bess, and then Will. The children were all close in age, a lot of mouths to feed and a lot of bodies to clothe.

In July 1897, Jennie gave birth to Miriam, who died at fourteen months. In December 1898, the family celebrated the birth of Simon, a comfort to replace the lost child—only to bury Simon at seven months. But soon Jennie was expecting again, and all the Congletons rejoiced, somewhat anxiously, in the birth of Jennie Whitley Congleton, named for her mother, on May 16, 1900. It was a hopeful way to start the new century.

The elder Jennie didn't have much time to enjoy her little namesake, who quickly became known as "Jennie Whit" to distinguish her from her mother. Jennie became pregnant again, and this time things went tragically awry. Jennie Whit was only two when her mother and the new baby died in childbirth on March 10, 1903. Jennie Whit's first memory was someone holding her up to a window to see her mother and the baby, stretched out on a bed in the house, awaiting burial.

A. B.'s response to the loss of his wife was to reorganize the household. Jim and Ed went to farm work. Bess, who was ten, was put in charge of the kitchen, with Will, now seven, in charge of Jennie Whit. Will wasn't that good a babysitter. One day he decided Jennie Whit needed a walk in her carriage. He threw her into the buggy and started trotting around the outside of the house. Jennie Whit seemed to like going fast, so he went faster and faster until at last they were fairly flying around the two-story farmhouse. But then the buggy got *too* fast. They were coming up on a tree, and Will couldn't turn out of the way in time. There was no choice but to save himself. He let go of Jennie Whit's buggy and hurled himself out of the way, leaving his sister to her fate. Luckily Jennie Whit was unharmed in

*Jennie Whit is the baby in Jennie Congleton's arms. Others are, from left, Jim, Will (wearing a skirt, as young boys did in the era), Bess, and Edwin, and father A. B.*

the ensuing crash, although Will no doubt took a licking for it. Despite the buggy crash, Jennie Whit and Will were close. Will was, along with Bess, the closest thing Jennie Whit had to a mother.

As they grew up, in fact, Bess and Jennie (as she often called herself now) worked out an interesting arrangement: Jennie went to work and Bess kept house for her. That went well for some time, until someone challenged Bess about being an old maid stuck waiting on her little sister. "You'll never leave this place unless *you* choose to leave," a friend told her. Bess realized this was so, and she pulled up stakes and moved to San Jose, California. This brought on a radical change for Jennie, and Albert saw his chance. He began seriously courting her, having probably met her at State Farm. If Albert had been worried about entering the dating scene again now that he had lost his hair, he didn't need to worry about Jennie's opinion. Her beloved brother Will was bald, too.

BESS HAD NOT BEEN in California for long before Jennie sprang the shocking news: she was thinking of marrying Albert Caldwell. He was fifty-two to Jennie's thirty-seven, but Jennie felt sure she could count on Bess's approval. Bess, she knew, liked Albert. Indeed, who didn't like Albert Caldwell?

At first, her family didn't. While they were dating, Jennie and Albert and another couple visited Jennie's oldest brother, Jim, and his family in Stokes. The other man was young and tall and good-looking, and the family thought (or hoped) Jennie was interested in him. There wasn't that much spare room in the house, so the family let the other man stay in a guest room and sent Albert to a boarding house in nearby Greenville. He hurried back for church the next day, too late for breakfast, and as a result ate at such an astounding rate for lunch that the slender Congletons were dumbfounded. Virginia, Jennie's small niece, was shocked when Albert lit into her mother's pickled peaches, a delicacy that the Congletons understood were meant to be eaten one per meal. He gobbled three.

Mainly, however, the Congletons were worried for Jennie's sake. Albert was divorced with two nearly grown boys. He had had that stroke. And there was the fact that he was fifteen years Jennie's senior. "You'll spend your life taking care of him," family members warned. When Jennie wrote home to tell everyone that she had accepted Albert's proposal of marriage, nine-year-old Virginia wrote back that when her daddy (Jennie's brother Jim) read that, "he got red and sweated." Likewise, Bess wrote to Jennie from California, "I got your letter yesterday. Was quite a little surprised to know that you are contemplating matrimony. I think Mr. Caldwell is a very nice man and anyway, tho' it is rather sudden if you should ever become dissatisfied it is quite fashionable to be divorced. Getting married is not as great a risk now as it used to be."

There was something Jennie was worried about: Albert was so well educated, and she was not. "You speak of Mr. C. being better educated than you," Bess reassured. "You are fairly well educated even if you don't have any degrees. Did you see in Winchell's column where Eddie Cantor who only got as high as the fourth grade in school was to address the Business class of Harvard University?"

Jennie and Albert were married December 22, 1936. Albert's sister, Vera, saw to it that Jennie, who suddenly needed to figure out how to run a kitchen, got a good cookbook and a bunch of Vera's recipes for Midwestern comfort food, ranging from Vera's Tuna Casserole to Vera's Apple Crisp. The happy couple wed in Richmond and as a very unusual honeymoon went to Rocky Mount, North Carolina, to admire Will's baby daughter, Kay, now about to turn 1. Albert found a lot in common with Will's wife, Dot, who was in-law to Jennie . . . but what was she to Albert? "I guess we're *out*laws," he teased, and ever after, the two "outlaws" called themselves that and vowed to stick together—which they sometimes did when the formidable matriarchs took charge of pickled peaches and other matters at family gatherings.

MEANWHILE, BACK IN THE Midwest, Sylvia was trying to keep a youthful Raymond on the straight and narrow. Raymond began drinking heavily. This must have been a deep disappointment to Sylvia, who had had such success guiding young men Christward in her Sunday School class back in her college days. She worried about Raymond's drinking, as did Albert from afar. The two were proud of maintaining a friendly divorce, although no doubt even a friendly divorce was hard on their sons and contributed to Raymond's drinking.

Perhaps to escape her troubles and to meet people after she became single again, Sylvia further developed her long interest in drama. She had started acting at Bloomington's Community Players from the time she had moved to Bloomington with Albert, and as the marriage faltered and then fell apart, she became a regular. She played Julia Rutherford in *A Little Journey*, Princess Beatrice's sister Symphorosa in *The Swan*, Mary Beal in *If*, Mrs. Pennington Brown in *Lombardi, Ltd.*, Mrs. Platt in *Up Pops the Devil*, and she played a lead role in the comedy *I Want a Policeman*. She had quite a stage presence, resulting in excellent reviews. She was lauded for throwing herself into her part in *A Little Journey*, and another reviewer of *A Little Journey* liked her performance so well that he said, "Mrs. Caldwell's wholesomeness in giving a sympathetic performance of her role was a beautiful piece of acting

*Sylvia on stage in* Lombardi, Ltd. *with the Bloomington Community Players. She is under the "A" in "Lombardi," playing the role of Mrs. Pennington Brown. The show was one of the greatest financial successes of the Players up until that time.*

and everyone will want to see her in another community play." Apparently everyone *did* want to see her in other plays. She was given a cameo publicity shot in the local newspaper when she was scheduled to appear in *Up Pops the Devil*, presumably because she was a good draw. *Lombardi, Ltd.* turned out to be one of the Community Players' greatest successes.

Meanwhile, Albert's mother and sister lived in Wisconsin, and Alden and Raymond still enjoyed the family lake house in that state. Albert made treks to the Midwest to visit that branch of his family. Even when the boys were grown, though, Sylvia was the one who had to deal mostly with their concerns, while Albert tried to parent from a great distance. Alden started college at Illinois Wesleyan University in Bloomington and graduated from University of Illinois in 1933 with a Bachelor of Science degree in chemical engineering. Raymond started at the University of Illinois but graduated from Illinois Wesleyan with a B.S. in business administration in 1937. He then went into the family business for the next twenty-six years, working for State Farm. He started as a code clerk in the fire insurance division and rose through various ranks, eventually becoming an underwriting superintendent.

Sylvia was an excellent secretary, a sharp cookie in a company where most of the female staff had not been college educated nor had been around the world. She stood out among them and was highly regarded. Whereas some of the young men in the firm thought it best to act as yes-men to their boss, G. J. Mecherle could count on Sylvia to be forthright. He could run ideas by her and get a straight-up, honest opinion.

Mae Mecherle died on August 22, 1942, and Sylvia and George were married a respectable year and a half later in Hot Springs, Arkansas, on January 8, 1944. They honeymooned at the Arkansas resort, a much different wedding trip than the journey to and aboard the *Manchuria* for Sylvia's first honeymoon. The fact that they married at all kept the gossips' tongues flapping about their relationship, but never mind. The former Sylvia Harbaugh Caldwell was proud to be Mrs. G. J. Mecherle now. She loved to give out her name as the wife of the State Farm founder. She saw herself as sort of a queen of Bloomington and truly enjoyed the role. She resigned her job at State Farm when she married, but she remained a leader among her circle. Executive secretaries would take social cues from her; according to one friend, if Sylvia ordered a cocktail at lunch, they would, too, even though G. J. Mecherle himself didn't drink (or didn't drink in public). Sylvia was definitely independent. And she was a stylish dresser and a gracious hostess.

George Mecherle had been a happy slave to his job, so Sylvia was determined that he learn to relax. As his biographer put it, because "State Farm was George Mecherle's one great interest in life he could hardly have chosen a more amiable or understanding companion" than Sylvia. But George was accustomed to listening to her, and she "quietly but firmly kept him from spending all his time and strength on his business affairs." He had almost never taken a vacation, other than a fishing trip each spring with fellow businessmen. In 1948, she talked him into a real vacation, his first in many years, and their first together other than their wedding trip to Arkansas. They took a cruise to the West Indies. It was the first time George had been at sea. To avoid seasickness, Sylvia picked a very large ship, the *Mauretania*

*Sylvia and her second husband, G. J. Mecherle, the founder of State Farm Insurance Co.*

*II*. She mentioned to the captain her link to the *Titanic*, and he asked if she would tell the story in an on-board lecture. It was so popular that she was asked to repeat it.

In 1949, the Mecherles went to Europe on a quest for George's family roots. George asked a travel agent to find the village of Untermasholderbach in Germany, where George's father, uncle, and aunt had lived before immigrating to America in the mid-1800s. Sylvia and George and two German guides researched George's long-ago family there. Afterward they reprised part of Sylvia's first European trip back in 1912. They went to England, although George was not so intrigued with palaces and cathedrals. He "was happiest when motoring through the farming regions," his biographer said, and that was how he enjoyed Europe.

Stateside, he and Sylvia also spent some time at Lac Court Oreilles in Wisconsin, at the old family lake house that Albert and Sylvia had bought and their children still used.

Sylvia succeeded in getting George to enjoy life in a more leisurely way, making their all-too-brief marriage pleasant and focused differently from his first. It was different from *her* first marriage, too, featuring an upscale and comfortable lifestyle that she loved. George was active until the last, dying suddenly on March 10, 1951, at age seventy-three, seven years after their marriage, leaving Sylvia a well-to-do widow.

SHE MIGHT HAVE LIVED on as the queen of Bloomington, but her life took a turn toward the national and even international spotlight in 1955, when she happened to come across an advertisement in the local newspaper. A historian named Walter Lord was seeking survivors of the *Titanic* to tell their story for a book he was writing, which eventually became the best-selling *A Night to Remember*. Sylvia answered the call. She told the story as she recalled it, traveling back mentally forty-two years or more to the mission posting in Siam, the trip through Europe, the decision to take the *Titanic*. She never mentioned her seasickness or the name of the illness that plagued her from Siam, nor did she discuss the symptoms that prevented her from carrying Alden off the ship. By then, neurasthenia had for many years been discredited as an illness, and it would have made her sound like a mental case to bring it up and to discuss her neurasthenia-induced inability to hold Alden, one of the critical factors in saving her first husband's life. Nor, of course, did she open any old wounds by suggesting she had left Siam under a cloud of suspicion. Such an admission would have muddied the reputation of the queen of Bloomington. She did, however, introduce a startling quote. She described how, when the *Titanic* was being loaded, she asked a baggage handler if the ship was really unsinkable. "Yes, lady," he told her, according to Sylvia's memory. "God Himself could not sink this ship."

Walter Lord was a careful researcher, refusing to use sensationalist details, no matter how juicy, without corroboration. Presumably he got the second witness he needed to the remarkable quote, because he used it. Maybe Albert corroborated it, or perhaps the deckhand did or someone else. In 1962, Albert recalled the quote as "Here is a boat that God Almighty cannot sink." Some have wondered why Sylvia kept such a spicy quote quiet more than forty years, thus questioning if it had been said in quite that way or even said at all. However, there was a slim bit of evidence from 1912 that tended to confirm it. On page 5 of Sylvia's 1912 *Women of the Titanic Disaster*, she referred to the *Titanic* as "the huge, almost defying work of man," which indicated the *Titanic* was defying God. Since the *Titanic* in and of herself was incapable of defiance, Sylvia's characterization of the ship as defying God indicated that she had heard someone defy God in the name of the *Titanic*—and perhaps "God Himself could not sink this ship" was that defiance.

No matter the exact origin of the quote, Sylvia's recollection of it as delivered in Walter Lord's book came to define the *Titanic*. The quote encapsulated and condemned man's feeble attempts to play God in claiming invincibility and in determining who lived and died that night. It was a theme that a former missionary approved of—especially a missionary who had been buffeted hard in the storms of her own life.

Her place in history now recorded by Walter Lord, Sylvia reigned on as queen of Bloomington. She was active in the Bloomington-Normal Art Association. She probably continued supporting (and maybe acting in) the Community Players in Bloomington for many years. As one of the social leaders of the community, the widow of G. J. Mecherle also served on the

*Sylvia posing with her copy of Walter Lord's famous history of the* Titanic, A Night to Remember. *A quote she recalled for the book, "God Himself could not sink this ship," became world-famous.*

*Sylvia, still stunning, photographed in the 1950s.*

Brokaw Hospital League and was a life member of the Bloomington Country Club. She was a member of the Order of the Eastern Star, and of course she was a member of Second Presbyterian Church.

Life was busy for Sylvia, revolving around her social position in Bloomington. She spoke sometimes about the *Titanic* and had a prepared opening and closing that she carried with her, but she gave the meat of the story from memory. Mrs. M. V. Mann, a survivor of the *Titanic* from Toronto, sent

Sylvia a "very fine letter" once. However, Sylvia lost interest in talking about the shipwreck. The past was another husband ago, a time now captured deftly in Walter Lord's book. She told her grandson about the *Titanic* only once, having gotten tired of talking about it. He didn't pay much attention; he was just eight years old. By 1963, Sylvia confided, "My doctor has advised me not to relive my experience" on the *Titanic*. She refused to answer her niece's questions about it.

ALBERT, ON THE OTHER hand, hoped to see the old ship again and to get his gold back. The gold had long since lost its taint; he no longer felt guilty about having saved the money, if indeed he ever had. He was fascinated at a Central Richmond Association meeting in 1959 when Retired U.S. Navy Admiral Dwight H. "Rainy" Day spoke about a submarine being developed by Reynolds Metal Co. that would hopefully withstand the extreme water pressure in the deep ocean. Day commented that the submarine, the *Aluminaut*, might one day find the *Titanic*. Albert couldn't resist the moment. "Admiral," he said, "I'm giving you a direct order. When you find the *Titanic*, I want you to find the $100 worth of gold I was bringing home from Siam. It's in the bottom of my trunk in the bottom of the *Titanic* at the bottom of the ocean!" As time wore on and neither the *Aluminaut* nor any other searcher had found the *Titanic*, Albert made sure the next generation would claim the gold. Jennie's beloved brother Will had died too young, and Albert had stepped in to become a surrogate grandfather to Will's granddaughters. The girls were enamored of the *Titanic* story and loved to hear Albert tell it. "When they find that boat and bring it up, you girls can have my gold pieces," Albert often promised them. Albert used to spend long stretches of time with Lloyd Hedgepeth, who married Will's daughter, Kay, working out the engineering of how anyone might raise the *Titanic*. "Do you think it's possible they could raise it?" he'd ask. "I'd like to see it again." Albert wondered if they could pump Styrofoam into the wrecked ship and float it. Lloyd was an engineer—not in undersea matters (he worked with the Air Force's space program), but that didn't stop Albert from speculating. He always knew they'd find the *Titanic*. He always knew they'd raise it. He hoped he lived to see the day.

*Albert got to ride through Richmond with star Debbie Reynolds as an advertising gimmick for the movie* The Unsinkable Molly Brown *in 1964.*

Albert enjoyed being a *Titanic* survivor. When the movie *The Unsinkable Molly Brown* came out in 1964, he got to ride around Richmond in a quaint Model T with star Debbie Reynolds. It was a promotional gimmick to advertise the movie, but Albert went along with it and rather enjoyed being seen riding with the famous and beautiful Miss Reynolds in her fur stole and white gloves, while a costumed chauffeur drove them through downtown. Albert saw the movie, too, and could quote every detail of it for the next dozen years. It was remarkable that he had met the real Molly Brown so long ago when she gave Alden a funny little garment to keep him warm on the *Carpathia*. Alden was now fifty-three.

Other than Sylvia and Alden, Albert never contacted another survivor until the early 1970s. He got in touch with a man who had been twelve at the time and who happened to be touring Virginia. And another survivor contacted him—a man from nearby Norfolk who was just a few days older than Alden. "Had an interesting visit with both," Albert reported in a Christmas card to *Titanic* historian Ed Kamuda.

During his life in Richmond, Albert became an elder in Grace Covenant Presbyterian Church and a member of Dove Masonic Lodge. After he retired from State Farm in 1958, he and Jennie moved into a retirement apartment in Richmond, and he served as president of the Richmond chapter of the American Association of Retired Persons. He entertained the retirees in his complex with things they might remember from the past—the *Titanic*, of course, but also "O, the Mistletoe Bough." Once an elderly lady remembered the creepy song fondly as an old favorite in her childhood. That pleased him a great deal. He also took up the ukulele, which he played enthusiastically.

He spoke about the *Titanic* to schools, lodges, church groups, clubs, whoever asked, and he never charged a fee—he was proud of that. Of course, he *had* charged to speak back in 1912 on the Chautauqua circuit, but those days were so many careers ago. Now he never charged, considering the telling of the *Titanic* story to be something of a public service. Near the end of his life, a church from the rougher side of the tracks with an all-black congregation asked him to speak. It seemed on the surface a scary proposition for an old man well into his eighties. "So I told them I'd do it for $25," he confided to his great-niece. "I thought they'd turn me down." But who wouldn't pay $25 ($123 now) to hear a *Titanic* survivor? The congregation came up with the money happily. "And you know what?" Albert said. "They were the nicest people I ever spoke to. Taught me a lesson!"

Jennie sometimes tagged along with him as he gave his speech, always having to fight the battle of explaining that she herself was not on the *Titanic*; that was the *first* Mrs. Caldwell. "Has anyone ever heard a survivor of the *Titanic* speak?" Albert would open the speech, and Jennie would grin wryly and raise her finger slightly, just out of Albert's range of vision. A talented artist, she once painted a picture of a ship leaving port, evocative of the *Titanic*, with the inscription, "Should auld acquaintance be forgot?"

Albert wrote to his sister, Vera, once a week in Wisconsin. He visited Wisconsin from time to time, where he helped Vera keep her house up, clipped favorite Midwestern recipes for Jennie, and kept up a chatty correspondence via mail with his wife. He was prone to write goofy love poems, too:

*Jennie Caldwell, who got pretty tired of hearing about the* Titanic, *painted this scene of a ship leaving port, likely meant to be evocative of the* Titanic, *although it was not an exact likeness.*

Here I am in Old Wis
And My dear wife I do miss.
But I'll soon be back
In our little shack
And give her a great big Kiss.
Heaps of Love
Your Hubby

When Albert wasn't visiting in Wisconsin, he was taking Jennie to various exotic destinations—the Holy Land, St. Augustine, Europe—and they even got to Italy, now cholera-free. These were places a small-town North Carolina orphan girl would never have dreamed of going. Her mother would have been thrilled. And Jennie need never have worried about her lack of education. She and Albert turned out to be a perfect match.

Back in the Midwest, Sylvia's health began to fail. She went into the Brokaw Hospital in Bloomington in November, 1963. She lingered for fourteen months, never leaving the hospital. Around New Year's, 1965, she had a stroke and then contracted pneumonia. She died January 14, 1965, at age eighty-one at 12:36 A.M. The Reverend Russell Shaw preached her funeral the following Saturday at the Metzler Memorial Home, and she

*Albert and Jennie Congleton Caldwell at St. Augustine, Florida.*

*Albert became the surrogate grandfather to Will Congleton's
grandchildren. Pictured here in Rocky Mount, N.C., circa 1965, he
watches over two of them.*

was buried in Bloomington in East Lawn Cemetery. Albert outlived her by a dozen years.

Contrary to all predictions in 1936, Jennie never did wind up taking up care of Albert; he wound up taking care of her. Jennie's delicate health, exacerbated by smoking, began to fail. Albert, then ninety, took great care to make her walk in the halls of their retirement complex every day. He himself did "squats" and other exercises in the hall each day to keep limber. His "outlaw," Dot, also in failing health, wrote him for his birthday in September 1976. He replied on the day he turned 91:

> Jennie is about the same . . . I cook her a good breakfast and bring her a good meal, from the cafeteria at noon . . . I make her walk, up and down the hall, every day . . .
>
> I am feeling fine and glad to be alive. My Mother died on her 91st birthday. She was incapacitated for the last ten years of her life and died in a Nursing home. If I can keep well for a few more years, I know I will not have to be in a Nursing home very long.
>
> With Love,
>
> Al

He had always joked with Dot about the "outlaws" sticking together, and in the end they did. Both of them died on the following March 10, Albert in the morning and Dot that afternoon, twenty-six years to the day after Sylvia's G. J. had died and seventy-four years to the day from when Jennie Whitley Congleton had died in childbirth and left Jennie motherless. And now Jennie was alone again. It was a strange coda to two families divided and united by divorce and remarriage. Jennie's family buried Albert in a place he had never lived, Greenville, North Carolina, near her childhood home, on March 14. Mourners heard a service at Grace Covenant Presbyterian Church in Richmond at 10 A.M., and the service changed states with the burial at Pinewood Memorial Park in Greenville that afternoon at 3:30.

*Albert as an old man, caught in a serious moment.*

# Phantom from a Watery Grave

Although both Sylvia and Albert were now gone, and although the *Titanic* had been gone many decades, it seemed the ship was not content to rest in its watery grave but instead haunted the Caldwells, even in death.

Truthfully, it had been haunting the Caldwells all their lives. It didn't seem so at first glance. As some relatives and acquaintances looked back over Albert's life, many recalled that he had always loved talking about the *Titanic*. He had always wanted his gold back, "as it would be worth a lot more than $100 today," he often mused. He usually seemed unhaunted by the ship. Then again, he once told a co-worker at State Farm that he wished he had never been on the ship or had even lectured on it or answered questions about it.

Indeed, part of Jennie's family found the same reaction. When Albert came into their lives, Jennie's nephew, Beverly Congleton, then seventeen, had read a book about the *Titanic* and was anxious to hear about it from his new Uncle Albert. However, Jennie asked Beverly's mother not to let him mention it. Beverly's mother concluded that Albert didn't like to speak of it. Of course, newlywed Jennie may have hoped the subject wouldn't come up. Why would the new wife want to hear about the adventures of the old one? That edict carried on over two generations in that branch of the family, so that Beverly's sons rarely heard the story because, apparently, they were not allowed to bring it up.

Over time Jennie felt secure in her marriage and got past the hesitancy to hear about Sylvia. Generally, therefore, Albert became known as a willing speaker on the *Titanic*. After Albert died, the *Richmond Times-Dispatch* said admiringly that he was an easy source, noting, "Unlike many of the 705 survivors who never wanted to speak of what they had endured,

Caldwell readily talked and wrote about the aftermath of the supposedly indestructible ship's almost matter-of-fact brush with an iceberg." Will's granddaughters—Jennie's great-nieces—always clamored to hear about the *Titanic*. Their mother, Kay, had been a baby when Jennie and Albert married, and it had never occurred to Kay that the children shouldn't ask about it. Albert told the story every time the girls asked. Kay had even had him down to Raleigh, North Carolina, to speak about the *Titanic* before all their friends, and Albert was thrilled to have a big audience.

Despite the fact that Albert had rarely allowed himself to be haunted by *Titanic* ghosts, it did seem the *Titanic* reached up from the depths to spook the Caldwell family in many other ways. Raymond, Sylvia and Albert's second son, born two years after the *Titanic*, was somewhat bedeviled by the fact that he alone of the family had not been on the ship. He was the odd man out when it came to the family's accidental place in history as *Titanic* survivors, a fact that was even pointed out in his funeral program when he died. He had a more anonymous life than the other members of his family. He went into the Navy in World War II, cruising the Pacific his parents had sailed on three and a half decades earlier and rising to the rank of lieutenant. He had a family, and a company newsletter described his home as centered "around his lovely wife Helen, and . . . enlivened by two delightful youngsters," Christine (who went by Chris) and Chuck. They were Albert and Sylvia's only grandchildren and went on to achieve much; Chris became a pediatrician, and Chuck earned a PhD in botany. Sadly, Raymond was overwhelmed by alcoholism when the youngsters were small, becoming a distant figure to them.

After Sylvia died, Raymond, or "Ray," as he was called by then, took stock of his broken life and decided it was time to change it. As his funeral program recalled upon his death in 1990, " . . .Ray said that while the Iowa vital statistics showed his birth as occurring in 1914, he considers his birth date to be February 1, 1969—the date he entered Michigan's Brighton Hospital. Ray was an alcoholic." He successfully kicked the alcohol habit at Brighton. His funeral program added, " . . .[L]ike his parents, Ray survived an almost tragic death. He started a new life! He went onto help create the McLean County, Illinois, Alcohol and Drug Assistance Unit and for ten years was one of Brighton Hospital's most effective and popular counselors." Ray's family had survived the *Titanic*, and Ray, too, was at last also lauded as a survivor.

The specter of the *Titanic* even materialized to haunt Chuck, Ray's son, when he was a child. About the time Sylvia fell ill for the last time, Albert visited Chuck and told him the story of the *Titanic* in great detail. Chuck, who was twelve at the time, retold it in school the next day for show and tell. The other kids ridiculed him for having a male relative survive.

ALDEN NEVER WAS INTERESTED in the *Titanic*. His main curiosity about family history was whether the relationship to John Alden could be proven. He never could confirm what a modern internet genealogy shows—that indeed, Abigail Alden, great-great-granddaughter of John Alden, married Ebenezer Byram, and their great-great-grandson was William F. Caldwell, Albert's grandfather. Thus, the Caldwells and Aldens were truly related, just as the family legend had said. Alden nevertheless was overshadowed all his life by the *Titanic*, and in fact, Alden came to regret his association with the *Titanic*.

Alden's growing negative feelings about the *Titanic* perhaps influenced Albert's story of the shipwreck over the years. Although Albert frequently said between 1912 and 1929 that his baby son had saved his life during the *Titanic* disaster, by 1934, Albert had shifted his emphasis to the stoker who insisted that Albert and his family get onto a lifeboat. Until that major shift in theme, the story varied in the details about how Albert got into Lifeboat 13, ranging from being ordered into the lifeboat to hold baby Alden to Sylvia pleading that her husband be allowed in the boat to help with the baby. Various historians have speculated that Albert changed details of his story to improve his image or justify his exit from the ship, and indeed this could have been the case. However, the variations were relatively minor ones on a similar theme—until he began spotlighting the stoker.

The overall thematic shift to the stoker, rather than Alden, as the key player came into focus as Alden aged. By the time Alden was a teen, no doubt he would have objected to being called a baby in his parents' newspaper interviews about the *Titanic*. Probably he took some ribbing for it

*Alden Caldwell as a young teen.*

from his friends. But even more so, by the time he became a young man and was subject to press interviews himself, he likely had already developed his distaste for the topic. When Albert moved to Richmond, Alden was twenty-two, an adult with his own opinions and, more importantly, his own life and his own privacy. At that point, Albert made the major shift in how he told the story, emphasizing the stoker's role over the baby's in saving his life that dreadful night, although both Alden and the stoker had had heroic roles. The shift in the story may have been a simple courtesy to the now grown Alden; maybe Alden didn't want to be harassed by the media about an event he didn't even remember.

Of course, by the time Albert shifted the focus of his *Titanic* narrative, he was single again. He likely didn't want to bring up the first wife and first family in a touchingly sentimental way. There was no sense in running off potential girlfriends.

But Alden's feelings probably did play a role, as indeed, Alden sincerely disliked the *Titanic*. It was disappointing for him to have led a life of quiet accomplishment in the field of chemical engineering with hobbies as diverse as fishing and painting, but to be remembered only for an ill-fated voyage that he took at age ten months. Once he was visiting Albert and Jennie in Richmond in 1971, and Jennie's niece Kay and her family came up from Raleigh specifically to get Alden's and Albert's signatures on their copies of *A Night to Remember*. Alden sat awkwardly in a corner as the others visited around. They all knew each other, but it was surreal to him. Here was his father's second family, most of whom he had never met. "Now, Alden," Albert joked, signing the books, "You make your X. You were a baby and didn't know how to write in 1912." Alden didn't think that was so funny. Would the ship never quit haunting him? He did sign the books . . . with his name.

Throughout his adulthood, Alden kept hitting his own iceberg when it came to his birth records. Early in his career during the middle of the Great Depression, he was thinking about pursuing a job as a chemical engineer with the federal government, but you had to be an American for that. His birth records had gone down with the *Titanic*, and thus it was not even clear he was a United States citizen. Someone suggested that perhaps his parents had registered his birth with the U.S. Consulate in Bangkok, something they had not done, much to their regret. Sylvia filed a legalistic document explaining the situation. It was no doubt nerve-wracking, as jobs were so scarce. To have the lack of official documentation of Alden's birth keep him from a job during the Depression surely weighed heavily on Alden and his parents. The problem became moot when Alden got a job with Lehigh Portland Cement Co. in Allentown, Pennsylvania, not far from Sylvia's brother, Milton, in 1937. Alden eventually rose to the rank of research chemical engineer there, retiring in 1968.

But after his mother's death, Alden was approaching retirement age and needed to apply for his Social Security benefits—and still, he had no birth certificate to prove his age. Albert swore out an affidavit about the lost birth records. It was such a bother! Albert regretted again not having registered his son's birth with the U.S. Consulate in Bangkok in 1911, and he rued the fact that Alden's baptism in Biggsville after the *Titanic* had not been officially recorded in church records. It had been so many decades ago, but still the *Titanic* was following Alden, who didn't even remember it.

Because Alden was one of the youngest *Titanic* survivors and, consequently, one of the last living survivors, reporters frequently tracked him down, although he couldn't tell them much. "When I was a child, I heard the story over and over again," he recalled for a Florida newspaper a year after the remains of the *Titanic* were found on the bottom of the Atlantic. "For years, my parents used to give lectures on their experience." To emphasize that he didn't recall a thing personally, he added, "They say that I slept through it all." The only other survivor besides his parents that Alden ever met was Frank Aks, who attended Albert's funeral in 1977. Aks was three days older than Alden. They didn't recall the ship at all, but the strange bond of the *Titanic* had brought them together some sixty-five years later.

In contrast to his father's long-ago hope of raising the ship, Alden thought the finders of the wreck should leave the *Titanic* at the bottom. His reasons were not those of reverence, as with some survivors. "There's no reason to raise it," he said. "If they did, we wouldn't really learn anything from it, it would just be a curiosity."

Despite Alden's stand-offish attitude about the *Titanic*, he was cordial to one of his stepmother's great-nieces, who came across the picture of the

*Alden Caldwell painted a harbor full of fishing boats for his father and stepmother in 1946.*

Caldwells on the *Titanic* among Albert's effects. She sent Alden a copy. He had forgotten it, although it did bring back childhood memories. It had once been a treasure, he admitted, and he dug up Ray's address so she could send him a copy, too.

In spite of many people saying Alden was withdrawn and hermit-like, he was kind to Jennie's great-niece. He gamely answered her questions—she had found some baby shoes pressed flat next to his mother's booklet on the women of the *Titanic*. Were the shoes his? Did he wear them off the *Titanic*?

*Alden Caldwell in his bathing suit at Lac Court Oreilles, Wisconsin.*
*Behind him on the dock is his sister-in-law, Raymond's wife, Helen.*

He had never heard of them. Maybe they were Jennie's, he guessed. After all, he had always been told he was wearing nothing but a steamer rug. "Surely you were wearing a diaper, too," she suggested, and he laughed at that.

"Well, I guess that would be right!" he said.

By then he was spending his retirement as a classic snowbird: Wisconsin in the summer at the old family house on Lac Court Oreilles, and Florida in the winter in the city of Largo. He had never married, but he did travel between the two states with his cat and his dog. People noted with some distaste that he let his beard grow (he, like his father, sported a bald head), but what were they to expect? Here was a bachelor living in a fishing cabin on a narrow strip of land between two lakes in his retirement, with only a cat and dog to answer to. He loved that life. He sent Jennie's great-niece a postcard of Whitefish Lake and Lac Court Oreilles, with the spot of his house marked on the picture. "I have frittered away the season up here and now it is about time to begin getting ready to go home," he commented cheerily as a man who thoroughly enjoyed retirement.

He was haunted by the *Titanic*, not as some of the adult survivors had been taunted by screams of the dying or guilt at having been saved, but haunted merely because he had had the misfortune to be a passenger on the ship's sole voyage. In the end he left a legacy that harked back to a time before the *Titanic*, something pretty hard to do when the *Titanic* had happened to him when he was ten months old. Park College, now Park University, where his parents had met, represented that time. He left a scholarship in Sylvia's name in his will. It seemed fitting that Alden would leave a legacy to young people in need of educational funding, exactly the thing that Park had done for his own parents. For all the differences that ultimately drove them apart, they had both loved Park. When he died in Florida on December 18, 1992, at age eighty-one, Alden left Park a generous $600,000 as the basis for the scholarship, which aided more than sixty students in its first five years. Alden's estate eventually gave Park University permission to use some of the fund to aid in several construction projects, including a new athletic complex and a waterfall feature at the campus's front entrance.

AFTER ALDEN'S DEATH, THE *Titanic* came back to torment Albert, even though Albert never knew it. He was now resting peacefully beside Jennie in Greenville and had been ever since Jennie died in 1980. The shocking ghost appeared in the newspaper in New Bern, North Carolina, not far from Greenville. According to the article, Christie's auction house in London had sold a watch that Albert had used to bribe his way off the *Titanic*.

That ugly apparition had materialized on November 5, 1998, when Christie's put up for sale in London an 18-carat gold pocket watch by Sutherland & Horne. The watch had been made circa 1876 and featured a white enamel dial with Roman numerals and gilt hands. It was even damaged a little, with a hairline crack by the number XII. It also featured engraving: "Presented to JAMES CALDWELL by the employees of the Pumpherston

Oil Co. Ltd on his leaving to take charge of the Mining Department at Deans, June 3rd 1896." According to Christie's, "James Caldwell passed the watch to Albert Caldwell, a relative, in the early part of the 20th-Century, Albert handed the watch to a member of the crew (coxwain? [*sic*]) aboard *Titanic* to obtain lifeboat seats for his wife, child and self, the crewman's son, Elliott C. Everett, left it to his neighbour on his death." Christie's went on with Lot Notes in support of this claim:

> [W]ere it not for the detailed inscription on the watch it would be difficult to prove where this watch had been at any given time. However, the strong proof of ownership by the Caldwells and subsequent implied transfer into another, unrelated, family is recorded in the official reports written by the American and British governments after the disaster. The Caldwell family are mentioned twice in the American version: in the list of saved Second Class passengers naming Albert, his wife Sylvia and their son Alden with their address listed as 2 Upper Montague Street, London; and also in the list of Second Class passengers rescued by *Carpathia* numbered 16-18.

Clearly this claim of relationship to the *Titanic* meant something to 383 would-be buyers; the watch was valued at £400 to £600 ($721 to $1,082 today) but was sold for £5,750 ($10,361 today).

Albert's family was startled. A bribe had never been part of the story. Albert had always held his head high when it came to the *Titanic*; he had not seemed embarrassed nor appeared to be hiding anything. And yet now the *Titanic* seemed to be calling him a cheater more than eighty-six years after the supposed bribe took place.

The bribe story seemed dubious. No eyewitness who recalled the night of April 14–15, 1912, described Albert entering the lifeboat by way of a bribe. Had it been true, such a sensationalistic story seems likely to have come out at the time, especially during the international hand-wringing that followed the shipwreck. To add to that, it would have been irregular indeed for a crewman to demand a bribe to put a woman and baby on the lifeboat. Women and babies had first pick of the seats. According to consistent accounts over the years, various other people pleaded to get Albert on the lifeboat, without him ever opening his mouth about it. In all these accounts, access was generally granted or even encouraged so that he could hold the baby.

Further research turned up no coxswain with the last name Everett. There was a crewman named Everett Edward Elliott, a trimmer in the engineering department, but he died on the *Titanic*, and his body, when recovered, did not have a watch in the pocket. Thus, no descendant of a neighbor could have gotten one from him.

Then there was the matter of the inscription to James Caldwell. No one among Albert's descendants knew of James Caldwell. The James Caldwell in the inscription lived in Scotland and worked for Pumpherston Oil Co. as manager of Woolfords Coal Mine in 1912. Indeed, during 1912, James Caldwell was battling destructive striking mineworkers at Woolfords. As a town website notes today, "Woolfords mine was badly damaged by a mob of angry miners when it continued to work during the national coal strike. Windows were broken, tubs were thrown down the shaft and fires started. The manager (James Caldwell) and some of his men managed to put out the fires." In fact, five miners went to jail following the very serious series of incidents. According to one source, the strike started in late February 1912 and stretched until April 11, 1912, the day after the *Titanic* sailed. Another source said the strike was settled on April 6.

It's not known today exactly when in 1912 James Caldwell fought the fires in the Woolfords mine, but it would have been before the strike was settled in April. While the strike was going on, it would have been very unlikely for him to leave the embattled mine in Scotland to visit relatives who were passing through some four hundred miles away in London—if Albert and Sylvia even *were* relatives. It is even more unlikely that the Scotsman would have met Albert either in Missouri or Siam. He could have mailed a watch to Albert, of course, but thus far no one has found any evidence that they were kin to each other or even knew each other.

Finally there are the "Lot Notes" by Christie's itself. Christie's said the "strong proof of ownership by the Caldwells" is based on the inscription to the Scottish James Caldwell and that the "implied transfer into another, unrelated family is recorded in the official reports written by the American and British governments after the disaster." However, the official reports as documented by Christie's consisted entirely of the listing of the Caldwells as among the saved Second Class passengers and the record of their address in London as 2 Upper Montague Street. The Caldwells never lived in London; they were only *staying* at 2 Upper Montague Street. That address was home to a rooming house called The Bansha, which overlooked Russell Square and the Hotel Russell. The Bansha in 1908 advertised "Good table. Electric light. Baths. Billiards," for 25 to 42 shillings per week ($127 to $213.32 per week today), inclusive. The rooming house was still called The Bansha in 1912, and in fact it was noted as the London address of an Irish Member of Parliament, Jeremiah MacVeagh, who was also the London correspondent for Belfast's *Irish News*. MacVeagh's younger sisters, Mary and Kathleen, ran the twenty-four-room house. As a politician, MacVeagh had argued against persecution of Presbyterians in Ireland. Perhaps the Caldwells knew of that stand via Presbyterian literature and sought out The Bansha. Although it's just a guess, perhaps MacVeagh was the unnamed "friend" who took the picture of the Caldwells on the deck of the *Titanic*. The Caldwells may have met the journalist at the "good table" at The Bansha and realized a common destination to the big ship. The *Titanic* was built in Belfast, after all, and MacVeagh may have been reporting on it for the Belfast newspaper. If MacVeagh had taken the picture, he could have easily gotten the Caldwells' forwarding address from his sisters, who had probably gotten it as part of the routine information gathered at check-in.

No matter how friendly they may have gotten with others at The Bansha, however, the Caldwells were only tourists stopping briefly. Clearly the assumption implied in the Christie's Lot Notes, that the Caldwells lived permanently at 2 Upper Montague Street (thus allowing them ample time to make contact with James Caldwell), was off the mark. The search at Christie's has turned up empty as well in regards to the owner of the watch and the basis for his or her claim to its relationship to the *Titanic*. The auctioneer who handled the sale has left Christie's. He could recall the watch but did not recall the name of the person who submitted it for sale, and that person, he said, would know the watch's provenance. He suggested Christie's might have records, but Christie's responded that it no longer had records as to the watch's owner prior to its sale.

Taking all the evidence as a whole, it seems that the watch-bribe story is mistaken, an insubstantial *Titanic* ghost that has arisen from the Atlantic, wrongly haunting a man who otherwise refused to let the ghost of the *Titanic* haunt him in life. Albert Francis Caldwell did not go down with the ship, but it seemed the ship, at long last, was determined to drag him below the surface.

THEN THERE WAS THE fact of the actual resurrection of the *Titanic*. Neither Albert nor Sylvia was still alive on September 1, 1985, when Robert Ballard and a team of French and American scientists found the *Titanic* on the bottom of the ocean. By the time Ballard found the wreck, it was too late for Albert to claim his gold, and in fact, the ship was in such tatters that even his scheme of pumping Styrofoam into the hull would not have worked. Albert never saw the ship again, although he had very much hoped to. The *Titanic* managed to thwart that wish of his by less than a decade.

But there was a touch of the poetic in the finding of the *Titanic*, in regards to the Caldwells, anyway. Somehow, it seemed appropriate that Ballard finally found the *Titanic* on the anniversary of Sylvia and Albert's marriage. It was also fitting that the lost liner was found just one week before Albert would have turned 100. It seemed right, in an odd way, a playful wink of history, that the long-forgotten anniversary and century birthday marked a strange new life for the *Titanic*.

That wink and slight nod of history's head was suitable, given the fact that the ghost of the *Titanic* hovered over the Caldwells even after their lives were over. Undoubtedly the most enduring way the *Titanic* haunted the Caldwells, however, was that it sealed Albert, Sylvia, and Alden as permanently together, one family of three, uninterrupted by Raymond, uninterrupted by divorce, uninterrupted by George, uninterrupted by Jennie. By sheer chance, Albert, Sylvia, and Alden had found their way into history and into never-ending rounds of media coverage that continued throughout their lives and have continued long after their deaths. Even though Sylvia was pleased to be the queen of Bloomington as Mrs. G. J.

Mecherle; even though Albert had found an ideal match in Jennie; even though Alden strived to distance himself from the shipwreck he could not remember, the *Titanic* reached up from the depths and encircled them all, a ghostly presence binding them forever as one of the rare *Titanic* families who were all saved.

To the world and to history, Albert and Sylvia would forever be young missionaries, married and with a baby named Alden, trying to save souls and to save themselves in one of the ocean's most harrowing tragedies.

# *Titanic* MEMORABILIA

Since I am Jennie Caldwell's great-niece, I never knew Sylvia. I met Alden once and spoke and corresponded with him a little bit toward the end of his life. But Albert—"Al," as I called him—I knew Al as well as I knew anyone in my family. Although I had seven first cousins more or less my own age on my father's side, I thought my coolest relative was the aged Uncle Al on my mother's side. My friends thought that was weird, and probably my cousins did, too, but Al was just so interesting.

I first became aware of the *Titanic* connection when we returned from a trip to our home in Dayton, Ohio, when I was a child. There had been a carnival at our local school, the brand new Monticello Elementary, and one of the prizes that everyone won was a colorful little walking cane. Why children would need a walking cane, I'll never know, and neither did our friend Jeanne Lucas, who used one of the prize canes to beat on the spindly tree in our front yard. She was doing this as we drove up, and she was singing as she beat the tree rhythmically, "It was sad, oh it was sad; it was sad, oh it was sad; it was sad when the great ship went down!" Dad was vaguely worried that Jeanne might damage the struggling little tree, but Mom turned to me and said gravely, "Julie, you had a relative on that great ship." This scared me a great deal.

Several years later a movie about the *Titanic* came on TV, and I feigned disinterest, retreating to the sun porch, where I surreptitiously watched the TV through the doorway to the living room. I was knotted up with fear the whole time. Someone in my family had been on that thing! It was a feeling I saw mirrored in my own son Alden years later when he approached me at age five as I was reading about the *Titanic*. Face flushed, voice nervous, he quivered, "Mommy? Was I on that ship?"

When my childhood family moved to North Carolina in 1970, we were within a quick drive to Aunt Jennie and Uncle Al's apartment, and now I got to know the story of the *Titanic* very well from Al himself. Better than that, though, I got to know the magical Al. He was truly a character, someone my sisters and I adored. He'd lay out nine magazines on the floor and pretend to be telepathic, a trick he had supposedly picked up in mysterious Siam. He could pick out the magazine you had thought of *every* time, to our amazement. He had also learned a devotional in Siam, and he wanted us to learn it. It was in the native religion of the Siamese, he warned, but it was very interesting. He got us all on our knees and had us chant, "O-wah!" Then we bowed. He led us into the second part of the chant: "Tah-goo!" We bowed again, all the way to the floor—that was particularly important. And then came the last part of the invocation. "Siam!" Al chanted, and we chanted with him, bowing with our noses to the floor. We repeated the bowing and chanting over and over again, faster and faster until the syllables all ran together and we figured out that it was a hilarious joke. Oh, Uncle Al *loved* that one!

My sisters and I all were promised the *Titanic* gold at various times and still joke about making good on that promise. In a way Al did leave me some lovely gold nuggets from the *Titanic*. When he died, Jennie moved to a nursing home and had her nieces and nephew break up their apartment for her. My mother (who was Jennie's niece), still grieving for her own mother, the "outlaw" Dot, grabbed a stack of papers to sort through, without giving much thought to it. She was just helping her cousins close the apartment. However, in that stack of paper goods, we found so much interesting family history—genealogy, photos, letters—and, my goodness, there was a photo of three people on a ship! The recent losses in our family suddenly seemed far away indeed. Could this be Al and Sylvia and little Alden on the *Titanic*?

We spent the next several weeks in detective work. The faces in the photo were in the shadows and hard to identify, but there were plenty of other clues to go on. The fashions were right, we noticed, for 1912. The weather matched up to pictures in books that had been taken on sailing day, another pointed out. Someone else observed that the man in the picture held his little finger like Al did, a little crookedly, as though it had been broken and not set properly. My father, the engineer, compared the thick cable visible behind the man in the photo and noted it was a much bigger cable than similar cables shown in photos of the *Carpathia*, which meant the ship the family was standing on was much bigger than the *Carpathia*. Known pictures of the *Titanic* in books showed the railing just as it appeared in the photo. We went to a local hobby store to consult the store's magnificent model of the *Titanic* and found the exact spot they were standing. Finally we took the picture to Jennie. We trotted out a lot of pictures we had found for her to keep if she liked. When we brought that one out, she snorted. "Oh, there's Albert on the *Titanic*. I forgot we had that old thing," she said, with the vague scorn of the second wife who had heard about the first wife with long, long patience. How did he get the picture? "A friend of theirs in London took it and sent it to them," Jennie said.

And I don't think I told Jennie, but we also found a copy of Sylvia's booklet *Women of the Titanic Disaster*, carefully saved by Albert all those years, with a little soft pair of booties flattened beside it. Were those Alden's booties on the ship? I have suggested here that they were, but that is admittedly just a guess based on circumstantial evidence. I have been able to ascertain that they are from the right era (they match a bootie in the Samford University Special Collections Department, worn by an American baby in 1907), and

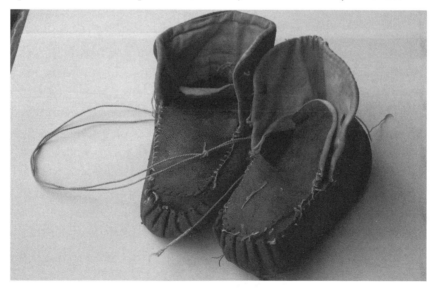

*Did Alden wear these shoes off the* Titanic?

they do fit babies at age ten months old (my own children tried them on at that age). Siam missionaries in 1911, when Alden was born, ordered their goods from the United States and Europe via a warehouse operation called "the Godown," run by Ed Spilman, so Albert and Sylvia could well have ordered them. The booties may have been bought in Europe on the way to the *Titanic* as well. However, we may never know for sure if they were Alden's. For all we know about the Caldwells' trip on the *Titanic*, many such questions are unanswered.

As much as I loved the *Titanic* story and as much as I have been intrigued by its mysteries, my most delightful memory of Uncle Al had nothing to do with the *Titanic*. We were taking the train from Washington, D.C., to Rocky Mount, North Carolina, where my grandmother—Al's "outlaw" Dot—lived. The train had a brief layover in Richmond, and my mother, Kay, had called Jennie and Al to let them know we'd be passing through their city. "Why, we'll meet you at the station!" Al said.

As the train rolled into Richmond, my sisters and I plastered our faces to the window, anxiously looking for Uncle Al. Would we see him? Would we find him in time? It seemed almost a crime that we might miss him. We only had a few minutes' layover.

But there he was! Uncle Al was on the platform, and he spotted us in the windows. This old man—he always looked over a hundred to me, although he rarely acted a day over thirty—started running, *running* to keep pace with our car as the train braked to a halt. He ran fast, fast, probably faster than I could run, and he anxiously held up something in his hands. We strained to see. Sandwiches! He had brought us pimento cheese sandwiches! He waved them toward our faces in the window, pointing at them in glee. Don't buy lunch, he was telling us, although we couldn't hear him. I have brought it to you!

I can still see him, from above, the joyous anxiety in my throat and the pimento cheese sandwiches raised heavenward. That was my Uncle Al.

I'm grateful to have been his niece.

# Sources of Information

## Firsthand Accounts

My first and most important source was my great-uncle Albert Caldwell. He never tired of answering my questions about the *Titanic*. About 1973 he came to Raleigh, North Carolina, where my family lived, and spoke before a large group of our friends and acquaintances. It was the same speech he had been giving since 1912. I remember the speech well, along with the in-depth conversation that followed at our house.

Albert left us a copy of his *Titanic* speech, written down at last in 1962 and last updated in May 1966. He titled the speech "They Said That the *Titanic* Could Not Sink." The Xeroxed typescript was a treasure of my childhood and is a treasure today. Even more of a treasure was the audiotape interview of Albert made by my mother's cousin Bill Romeiser, about 1976. It is still good to hear Albert's voice telling the story of his missionary service in Siam and his trip home via the *Titanic*.

When Albert died, family memories of what he had told us became important. I consulted his second wife, my great-aunt Jennie Whit Congleton Caldwell, about various aspects of Albert's story. My father, Lloyd Hedgepeth, had heard Albert's *Titanic* engine room story so many times that Dad could describe nearly every piece of equipment. Dad and my mother, Kay Congleton Hedgepeth, remembered parts of the *Titanic* story that I had forgotten, as did my sisters, Jan Wright and Anne Hedgepeth, and cousins Virginia Romeiser, Vera Congleton, and Jim Congleton.

The Caldwells' grandson, Chuck Caldwell, also recalled the *Titanic* saga as told by his grandparents. Besides offering some memories of their *Titanic* story that I had not heard, Chuck spent much time reconstructing the Caldwells' movements about the *Titanic* on the night of the sinking in excellent detail, using Sylvia's and Albert's accounts as a basis.

## Artifacts

Items belonging to Albert Caldwell that were passed down through my family revealed much about his life, including his high school graduation program and many family photos.

By far the most exciting artifact Albert left was the photo of the Caldwells on the deck of the *Titanic*. Other photos were kindly loaned to me. Chuck Caldwell supplied family photos of Albert, Sylvia, and Alden at many stages in their lives. Many college-era photos of the Caldwells came from Park University's Fishburn Archives, courtesy of archivist Carolyn McHenry Elwess. Photos of the Caldwells and their friends Bess and Sam Conybeare were loaned courtesy of Anne Conybeare Trach and Marcia A. Trach, the Conybeares' daughter and granddaughter. The Trachs also let me copy a postcard, picturing the *Titanic*, which Albert sent to Sam Conybeare after the *Carpathia* safely docked in New York. John Robertson furnished a stunning photo of the Caldwell family taken shortly before they left Siam, handed down from his grandfather, Dr. C. C. Walker. State Farm Insurance Company archivist Dan Barringer loaned photos of Sylvia and her second husband, G. J. Mecherle. My mother, Kay Congleton Hedgepeth, let me use the Congleton family photo taken outside their old farmhouse.

It was amazing what turned up in old scrapbooks and boxes of mementos. Bruce Parrish, historian of the Bloomington (Illinois) Community Players Theatre, patiently went through scrapbooks to find playbills, photos, reviews, and news clips of Sylvia's performances on stage. Dan Barringer at State Farm located Christmas cards sent by Albert to his customers that showed which companies he worked for, an area that had been very unclear before. In my own family's closet, I found many Congleton family artifacts, including Jennie Whitley's school essays and her doodled-in Latin book, as well as A. B. Congleton's teaching certificates. I also came across Jennie's recipe collection, which offered interesting insights about Albert and Jennie's life together. Someone in the Congleton family passed along the funeral program for Raymond Milton Caldwell.

Alden's and Jennie's paintings are owned by my mother, who graciously took them off the wall to be included as illustrations in this book.

## Documents
Many documents were critical in telling the Caldwells' story. The

Caldwells' files at the Presbyterian Historical Society (PHS) were key to their personal history and how others perceived them. Sylvia's personnel file there is designated as RG 360-24-24 and Albert's as RG 360-24-23. The files didn't say why the pair resigned from their missionary work in Bangkok, but microfilm from the PHS's secretarial files revealed that information and the rich story around it. That roll of film is labeled "Secretaries' files: Siam (Thailand) mission, 1865–," call number MF NEG. 170 r.3.

Sylvia Caldwell Mecherle's letter to *Titanic* researcher/author Walter Lord was quoted in "Sylvia Caldwell, Second Class Passenger" on Paul Lee's website, http://www.paullee.com. Sylvia quoted with an accent the man who famously told her the *Titanic* was unsinkable: "Yes lidy God himself . . ." The quote has been so often repeated as "Yes, lady," that I used that format. So many other letters also helped round out the story. John Robertson, Dr. C. C. Walker's grandson, still has a letter from Albert, written to Walker from the *Carpathia*. The text of the letter was passed along to me courtesy of Don Lynch and George Behe. Mr. Robertson was kind enough to clarify a few points based on the original letter. Carolyn Elwess of Park University furnished a letter from Addie B. Wyeth to an unnamed friend shortly after the *Titanic* in 1912, which was charming in its forthrightness about Sylvia's personality. Carolyn also copied an important letter from Joseph E. McAfee to Lowell McAfee, April 19, 1912, about the Caldwells' arrival on the *Carpathia*.

Other letters that played a part in this book included Albert's undated hand-written poem to Jennie, a letter from Jennie's sister Bess Congleton circa December 1936, and a letter from Albert to Dot Congleton on September 8, 1976, all in my own collection. *Titanic* historian Ed Kamuda passed along a Christmas card from Albert to Ed, circa 1972, and a letter from Sylvia to Ed, September 6, 1963.

Carolyn Elwess shared many other types of documents, including an affidavit by Albert regarding Alden's family tree, in order to affirm that Alden was a U.S. citizen; Alden's at-last-granted citizenship papers; and death certificates for Sylvia, Albert, and Alden. Another key affidavit came from my own collection. It was by Albert's mother showing that Stella Caldwell was his adoptive sister, not his natural sister.

*Titanic* historian Walter Lord corresponded with me over many years. He confirmed that the *Titanic* story as I heard it from Albert was as he had heard it as well. He authenticated the photo of the Caldwell family on the deck of the *Titanic*. Lord also owned a letter from Mary Hewlett to Marcia (no last name given), 30 May 1912, available through Dr. Paul Lee's website.

Alan Ruffman and Garry D. Shutlak furnished a key work, "Undated Recollections of Mrs. Henry Reginald Dunbar Lacon (née Hilda Mary Slayter; April 5, 1882–April 12, 1965)," c. late 1950s, which is Hilda Slayter's unpublished memoir. It was found and transcribed by Ruffman with the aid of Shutlak, Senior Reference Archivist, Nova Scotia Archives and Records Management, Halifax. I am grateful that Shutlak passed along the memoir to Chuck Caldwell and allowed me to use it.

Testimony by *Titanic* crewmen Frederick Barrett, George W. Beauchamp, Reginald Lee, and Frederick D. Ray, all on the *Titanic* Inquiry Project (available on the internet), were of high value. That website in general was an excellent source.

Brian J. Ticehurst unearthed American Red Cross, "No. 65 (American)," *The Emergency and Relief Booklet*, 1913. This source, supplied by Ticehurst to Chuck Caldwell, gives a listing of goods lost by one family on the *Titanic*. The booklet describes the applicant for relief as a missionary as returning from Siam with an invalid wife and infant daughter. Apparently the Red Cross's notation about an infant daughter was in error; surely this described the Caldwells.

Garry Shutlak supplied R.G. 41 Series C Volume 76A Coroner's Records, Nova Scotia Archives and Records Management, Halifax, regarding a crewman possibly associated with the watch-bribe story. Chuck Caldwell kindly passed this along to me.

Chuck Caldwell's family trees, traced through Ancestry.com, were invaluable.

One piece of oral documentation was of great help. Dan Barringer of State Farm Insurance passed along a story told to him by a former worker, which illustrated the strong moral stand taken by G. J. Mecherle in matters of office romances.

## PUBLISHED MATERIALS

When Albert died, I discovered among his effects an extremely rare short booklet, *Women of the Titanic Disaster*, written by "Mrs. A. F. Caldwell" and published in St. Joseph, Missouri, by A. W. Themanson Publishing, 1912. The booklet was a godsend in letting me hear Sylvia's voice. Much of her description of the lifeboat and the *Carpathia* comes from that source.

Albert and Sylvia themselves bought in 1912 a copy of Marshall Everett's *Story of the Wreck of the Titanic: The Ocean's Greatest Disaster—Memorial Edition* (L. H. Walter, 1912).

Several publications from Park College, including the *Park College Stylus* and *Park Alumniad*, all courtesy of Carolyn Elwess, were gold mines of information. These publications gave a well-rounded picture of Sylvia Harbaugh and Albert Caldwell as students and then as a young married couple. Many of their first-person accounts were quoted verbatim in Carolyn's own privately published article about the Caldwells, "Just as the Ship Went Down" (1998). She also wrote the privately published "The *Titanic* Resurfaces" (2010), based on those firsthand accounts. Carolyn located and transcribed key 1912 articles from the *Platte County Gazette* (Missouri) that otherwise would have been hard to find.

Washington Dodge's speech to the Commonwealth Club of San Francisco, May 11, 1912, was republished in the *Union Democrat* (Sonora, Calif.), on July 10 1998. Dodge quoted an article from a Roseville, Illinois, newspaper that reportedly ran April 26, 1912. No one has been able to locate a copy. However, archivist Heather D. Richmond of Western Illinois University unearthed the *Monmouth* (Illinois) *Daily Atlas* story of April 24, 1912, "Common Sailors Heroes of *Titanic*, Say Survivors." Fortunately, it largely parallels Dodge's quotes from the Roseville publication.

Ruth Becker's first-person narrative from Lifeboat 13 was useful. It is quoted in both "Ruth Becker: Child, Survivor, Heroine," http://Titanic-children.webs.com, and in "Ruth Elizabeth Becker Blanchard," http://www.angelfire.com/biz6/RuthBeckerBlanchard/story.html. I thank Don Lynch for clarifying Ruth's story and eliminating some mistakes I had included about her.

Articles with accounts by Percy Thomas Oxenham and Elizabeth Dowdell, published on the Encyclopedia Titanica website, was very helpful. Indeed, that entire website had much valuable information.

## BOOKS

Lawrence Beesley, *The Loss of the S.S. Titanic* (Boston: Houghton Mifflin, 1912; reprint, 2000); also, Beesley's testimony, "Testimonies of Healing," *Christian Science Sentinel*, 20 December 1913, p. 314.

Charles Edwin Bradt, William Robert King, and Herbert Ware Reherd, *Around the World: Studies and Stories of Presbyterian Foreign Missions* (Wichita, Kansas: The Missionary Press, 1912).

Daniel Allen Butler, *Unsinkable: The Full Story of the RMS Titanic* (Cambridge, Mass.: Da Capo edition, 2002).

Eric Caren and Steve Golman, *Extra Titanic: The Story of the Disaster in the Newspapers of the Day* (Edison, NJ: Castle Books, 1998).

Donald Hyslop, Alistair Forsyth, and Sheila Jemima, *Titanic Voices: Memories from the Fateful Voyage* (New York: St. Martins' Press, 1998).

Walter Lord, *A Night To Remember* (New York: Holt, Rinehart and Winston, 1955).

Don Lynch, *Titanic: An Illustrated History* (New York: Hyperion, 1992), and "Alden Gates Caldwell: *Titanic* Survivor," *The Titanic Commutator* 17, no. 2 (August–October 1993): 29.

Logan Marshall, 1912 *The Sinking of the Titanic* (abridged, edited, and reprinted in 1997 by Bruce M. Caplan, Seattle Miracle Press).

W. H. Sheridan McGlumphy, *Directory: Tax-Payers, Caldwell County, Missouri* (Kingston, Mo.: March 1906).

E. E. O'Donnell, *The Last Days of the Titanic: Photographs and Mementos of the Tragic Maiden Voyage* (Niwot, Colo.: Roberts Rinehart, 1997).

Violet F. Rowe, *Images of America: Glenshaw* (Charleston, S. C.: Arcadia, 1977).

Karl Schriftgiesser, *The Farmer from Merna* (New York: Random House, 1955).

Rev. Elisha B. Sherwood, *Fifty Years on the Skirmish Line* (Chicago: Fleming H. Revell, 1893).

Robert E. Speer, Dwight H. Day, and Dr. David Boviard, *Report of*

*Deputation of the Presbyterian Board of Foreign Missions to Siam, The Philippines, Japan, Chosen, and China* (New York: Board of Foreign Missions of the Presbyterian Church in the U.S.A., 1916).

Walter Williams, ed., *A History of Northwest Missouri* 3 (n.d.).

## PERIODICALS:

George Behe passed along a wonderful, revealing set of 1912 newspaper articles about the Caldwells from the *St. Louis Globe-Democrat* (Missouri), the *Washington Post* (Washington, D.C.), the *New York Sun*, the *New York Herald*, and the *Pittsburg Daily Dispatch*. (That Pennsylvania newspaper's name did not feature the "h" that is now customarily part of the word "Pittsburgh.")

Another key source was Bill Kemp, librarian and archivist with the McLean County Museum of History in Bloomington, Illinois, who sent an excellent set of interviews of the Caldwells over the years that appeared in the *Bloomington Pantagraph*. Their first-person accounts—some by Sylvia, some by Albert, some by both—were central to the unfolding of the story.

Important articles on Albert's Chautauqua experience appeared in the summer of 1912 in the *Holt County Sentinel* (Oregon, Missouri), preserved by the Library of Congress.

Also, Dan Barringer of State Farm Insurance furnished many contemporary articles from company newsletter *ALFI*, which were particularly helpful in discussing the careers of Sylvia and her son Raymond.

An obituary for Caroline Sweetser Howard Dennis from an unnamed Iowa newspaper, located on Ancestry.com by Paula Noles, answered the nagging question of who Stella Caldwell's natural parents were. Jacky Johnson at Miami University of Ohio delved into Western College publications and documents to discover further information on Stella for me.

Other useful articles came from various newspapers, including the *Cedar Rapids Daily Republican* (Iowa); the *Evening Tribune* (Ames, Iowa); the *Richmond Times-Dispatch* (Virginia); the *Richmond News-Leader* (Virginia), the *Pittsburgh Press* (Pennsylvania) and the *St. Petersburg Times* (Largo-Seminole edition, Florida).

Missionary periodicals that were of help included the *Annual Report of the Board of Foreign Missions of the Presbyterian Church in the United States of America* for multiple years, *Seventy-Fifth Anniversary Series: Siam and Laos, The Missionary Review of the World,* and *Women's Work.*

## Controversies and Educated Guesswork

As I noted in the introduction to this book, the Caldwells' story was sometimes thick and full of texture due to abundant firsthand accounts, and other times it was spindly for lack of solid evidence. In some of the more spindly places, I was able to discuss various debatable issues in the text. In other cases, however, the discussion was too unwieldy or unreadable in the context of the story, so I discussed the debatable points in the footnotes. Those footnotes are available through www.NewSouthBooks. com/raretitanicfamily/sources, but since they don't appear here, I will sum up sources on some of those lurking questions:

Was Sylvia really sick? All the years I was growing up, I heard the rumors in my family that Sylvia faked an illness to leave Siam. We didn't know Sylvia, and our suspicions were tainted by that fact. After much searching, I found through the records of the Presbyterian Historical Society that she had been diagnosed with neurasthenia, and when I researched what neurasthenia was, the rumors began making sense. The disease was once popularly diagnosed but became discredited many years ago. I found out much about the disease's rise and fall from the medical lexicon via sources including Frank K. Hallock, MD, "The Sanatorium Treatment of Neurasthenia and the Need of a Colony-Sanatorium for the Nervous Poor," *Boston Medical and Surgical Journal* 164, no. 3 (19 January 1911): 73-77; Ruth E. Taylor, "Death of Neurasthenia and its Psychological Reincarnation: A Study of Neurasthenia at the National Hospital for the Relief and Cure of the Paralysed and Epileptic at Queen Square, London, 1870–1932," *The British Journal of Psychiatry* 179 (2001): 550-557; Richard N. Fogores, MD, "Dysautonomia: A Family of Misunderstood Disorders," About.com Guide; and Tom Lutz, *Doing Nothing: A History of Loafers, Loungers, Slackers, and Bums in America* (New York: Farrar, Straus, and Giroux, 2006). These sources ranged from actual case studies of physical symptoms of neurasthenia in Taylor's study to Lutz's contention that neurasthenia was a form of loafing. Medical historian Mike Flannery of University of Alabama at Birmingham scoffed at the diagnosis because "neurasthenia" was too blanket a term; it could have meant lots of things.

It was intriguing to find out what the treatment was for neurasthenia in Frederick A. McGrew, MD, "Neurasthenia and the Rest Cure," *Journal of the American Medical Association* 34 (1900): 1466-1468. I saw some historic evidence of that treatment at one of the Flagler hotels in St. Augustine, Florida, recently. A Turkish bath there catered to people who were in Florida for their health around the turn of the twentieth century, including those with neurasthenia.

Most critical of all in determining whether Sylvia was really ill was a *Line a Day Diary* penned by Siam missionary Bess Conybeare (Elizabeth M. Furniss Conybeare). The diary was furnished by Anne and Marcia Trach. Bess's diary showed that Sylvia truly was ill much of the time.

**DID THE CALDWELLS TRY TO TAKE THE** *Carpathia* **HOME FROM NAPLES?**
Pieces of this interesting puzzle have only recently fallen into place. Albert's niece and her husband, Kay Congleton Hedgepeth and Lloyd Hedgepeth, recalled that the Caldwells considered taking the *Carpathia* from Naples— "without a doubt," Kay says. Anne Hedgepeth, Albert's great-niece, recalled the same thing, remembering that Albert actually went to the ticket office to book the *Carpathia*. My childhood memory was that Albert got onto the *Carpathia* and looked it over, speaking to sailors aboard, although no one else recalls that. I always had the idea that he thought about taking the *Carpathia*.

Meanwhile, the Caldwells' grandson, Chuck, had the impression that Sylvia insisted they take a large ship, perhaps even after they had bought tickets on another vessel, although he did not think it was the *Carpathia*.

Admittedly, Albert's tape says he merely asked the name of the ship and did not mention a desire to take the *Carpathia*.

Chuck Caldwell recalled from childhood that Albert said they became afraid of cholera, somehow spurring their journey home. Chuck always associated that fear with leaving Siam, but the mission records now in the Presbyterian Historical Society show no concern about cholera and show that Sylvia had been diagnosed with neurasthenia.

Then I came across a key book, Frank M. Snowden's *Naples in the Time of Cholera, 1884–1911* (Cambridge, UK: Cambridge University Press, 1995). The book makes clear that cholera was a big problem in Naples—which was exactly where the Caldwells had planned to take the "rest cure" for Sylvia's neurasthenia. Knowing that the Caldwells' plan was to spend some time in Naples, I am guessing that discussion of the ongoing 1911 cholera outbreak, just coming to public light, caused the young family to cancel their Naples plans in a hurry.

It makes sense, then, that the Caldwells might have seriously considered fleeing Naples on the first available ship, which happened to be the *Carpathia*. The *Carpathia* was in Naples on March 14, 1912. See Istria on the Internet, "*Carpathia*," istrianet.org. The ship left the next day, according to "List or Manifest of Alien Passengers for the United States: S.S. *Carpathia*, sailing from Naples, 15th March 1912." I'm grateful to Chuck Caldwell for copying the Immigration Service manifest to me.

It would seem to be a big question as to why the Caldwells would be able to throw together a European trip on the spur of the moment after they decided cholera rendered Naples unsafe. However, a letter to the editor of *Railway Age Gazette* of Oct. 18, 1912, offered insight. According to the letter-writer, a trip to Europe was economical and was considered to be a destination for people of moderate or even poor means.

**DID ALBERT REALLY TRY TO BRIBE HIS WAY OFF THE** *Titanic*? No report from the era ever mentioned Albert bribing his way off, and it seems likely it would have come out if he had done so. It was legitimate for men to be on the lifeboats—Lawrence Beesley and Washington Dodge were already aboard 13 when the Caldwells arrived, so no bribe was needed. Beyond that, though, I have pieced together evidence against the bribe theory.

The allegation of a bribe came to my attention via my cousin, Jim Congleton, who had clipped an article by Scripps-Howard News Service, "*Titanic* Fever Pushes Up Auction Sales Prices," c. November 1998 from a New Bern, N. C., newspaper. It told of a watch that Albert supposedly gave a crewman to get the family off the *Titanic*. The watch had recently been put up for auction. The article seemed to believe that the Caldwells lived in London at 2 Upper Montague Street. Indeed, that is the address they gave—see "Exhibit B—Alphabetical List of Second-Class Passengers on Steamship '*Titanic*,' April 10, 1912," in *"Titanic" Disaster: Report of the Committee on Commerce, United States Senate* (Washington: Government Printing Office, 1912), p. 50. And yet, we know for a fact that the Caldwells did not live in London. Clearly the list came from the White Star Line, as Albert would have given this temporary address as he waited for a hoped-for ticket cancellation.

Proof that this was not a permanent address for the Caldwells came from, of all places, a book designed to teach English to non-English speakers by having them read newspaper advertisements. In Louis Hamilton, *The English News-paper Reader* (Leipsic: G. Freytag, 1908), the advertisement reprinted on p. 260 showed clearly that 2 Upper Montague St. was a rooming house called The Bansha and catered to tourists. It's clear 2 Upper Montague Street was still a rooming house called the Bansha in 1912, based on sources of the day.

I consulted Christie's auction house about the watch, which Christie's sold in sale number 8182, lot number 32. Christie's described the watch as coming to Albert from a relative, James Caldwell of Woolfords, Scotland. I received cordial responses by email from Emily Fisher of Christie's. Christie's also directed me to Charles Miller, the auctioneer who had handled the sale. I found via those contacts that Christie's had no further record of the sale nor any further information on the watch.

Research showed that James Caldwell was actually fighting fires set by striking miners at his coal mine in 1912. His frantic efforts to put out fire at his mine are mentioned in "Woolfords Coal Mining," Woolfords History, http://www.forth.themutual.net/woolfordshistory.html. The coal strike either ended four days before the *Titanic* sailed or one day after, depending on the source giving the information. Even if it ended a few days before the *Titanic's* sailing date, it would have been very unlikely for James Caldwell to have gambled that all really *was* settled and that miners would not set the place on fire again while he made a mad dash to see relatives in London and pass along a watch to them. True, James Caldwell could have mailed the watch to Albert or, less likely, visited him in Bangkok or Missouri. As of now, however, we can't find a relationship between James and Albert. It seems the bribe story is, therefore, a mistake of some sort.

Interestingly, Albert's great-nephew Jim Congleton said that when he read the watch-bribe article, he recalled Albert saying he had left his watch on the bedside table on the *Titanic*. I recalled Albert saying he left money in a box at bedside, although I don't recall a mention of a watch.

WHY WAS LIFEBOAT 13 STUCK? Albert and Sylvia both reported on Lifeboat 13 being stuck fast to the side of the *Titanic*, resulting in Lifeboat 15 descending on top of 13, so close that the frightened occupants of 13 beat on the bottom of 15. At that point, crewmen Frederick Barrett and Robert Hopkins cut 13's ropes with a knife, thereby freeing the lifeboat from the *Titanic*.

There is a disagreement as to why 13 was stuck. Lawrence Beesley, in his book, said the release mechanism was a pin that had to be tripped. It was small and hard to find, and the crew was not familiar with the mechanism. That may be so.

However, Albert said in his audiotape and in his speech that a lever designed to release the lifeboat's block and tackle was gummed up with red paint. The color was seared into my memory as a child, because it had never occurred to me before then that the *Titanic* was in color. I was kind of embarrassed about how silly I had been to think of the ship as being black and white only, like her photographs. The color issue was seared into my sister Anne's memory as well, as she recalled the mechanism as being gummed up with "*shiny* red paint," according to Albert's description. Whenever Uncle Al described this to us, he would pretend to be pulling an imaginary lever. Albert also referred to paint gumming up the mechanism in interviews with the press in Richmond, Va., where he spent the latter part of his life. See "A Trunk on the *Titanic* Contains Some of Albert Caldwell's Gold," *Richmond Times-Dispatch,* 7 September 1985. After the *Titanic* was found at the bottom, the *Times-Dispatch* rounded up various articles in which

Albert had been interviewed over the years and quoted them. He clearly had mentioned the paint in those newspaper reports.

A lever did not square with a small, hard-to-find pin. There was some question as to whether Albert could see the color in a pitch black night with no moonlight and no light on the boat. It is possible, of course, he observed the color as dawn broke or afterward.

The question of whether 13 was stuck by a hard-to-find pin or a painted-over lever isn't settled by this, but it's clear that Albert did perceive of a painted-over lever as the culprit.

How rare was this Rare *Titanic* Family? Using the passenger lists on Encyclopedia Titanica, I counted groups of people with the identical last names and assumed each last name constituted one family group. I then consulted the survival list and saw how many of those original groups arrived in New York intact. Obviously, this method has some flaws. Members of the same family could have had different surnames, or multiple people with a common last name might have represented more than one family. Thus, my estimate that only ¼ of *Titanic* families survived intact is an educated guess. It's probably a good rough estimate, but it is only rough.

Were the baby shoes Alden's? When Albert's effects came to my mother, among them were a pair of soft leather baby booties smashed flat against Albert's copy of Sylvia's *Women of the Titanic Disaster*. The booties and booklet appeared to have been saved together. I have always hoped the little shoes were stored there because they were Alden's booties that he wore off the *Titanic*, although I've been unable to find the answer. I *can* say that I've tried. The booties fit a baby at age 10 months (I tried them on my own children). I consulted a University of Alabama professor whose expertise was old clothing. He said they were probably of the right era, as they featured machine stitching and hand-work, but he couldn't discern anything further.

Lawrence Beesley in his book reported that Alden's toes were "exposed," so Beesley covered them with a blanket. That could have meant Alden kicked off a blanket to expose his toes (with his feet still clad in booties) or kicked off a bootie (resulting in exposed toes) or had never been put in shoes at all but had wiggled his toes free of the blanket he was wrapped in.

However, having been outside to check on the situation after the collision with the iceberg, Albert knew how extremely cold it was. It stands to reason he and Sylvia would have put Alden's shoes on him if the shoes were not in the locked trunk. They probably were not, as Alden seems to have lost the keys to the trunk earlier in the day and would have probably been wearing shoes at the time he lost the keys. Maybe the baby even wore the shoes in bed, as they were soft, not hard-soled. As an adult, though, Alden, had never heard of a pair of shoes related to the *Titanic*. Alden wondered if perhaps the shoes belonged to his stepmother, Jennie.

After the advent of the internet, I found a similar pair of shoes on the web page of the Wisconsin Historical Society. The Society didn't know much about them, but felt they were modeled after Indian moccasins sometime between 1850 and 1900. The booties, they felt, were clearly designed to Midwest taste. Would such things have been sold in Siam? The Society doubted that.

Then I had a breakthrough in the archives at Samford University in Birmingham, Alabama, while looking through the papers of former university president A. P. Montague. An envelope fell out labeled something like, "Evelyn's baby shoe—a souvenir of a lovely baby." The shoe in the envelope, though designed for a female newborn (it featured a pink ribbon), was virtually identical in construction to my shoes. I found that Evelyn had been born in Alabama in 1907—four years before Alden. In that case, the shoes were more of Alden's era than his father's (Albert was born in 1885). But would a baby in Siam have owned such a shoe? In time I found an account by Ed and Daisy Spilman in the Presbyterian Historical Society microfilm. Ed ran "the Godown," a warehouse type of affair where all the goods missionaries would need were imported. Most of these goods came from America or Europe. So it is possible, then, that the shoes were imported via the Godown, or perhaps bought in Europe on the way to the *Titanic*, or maybe given to Alden as part of the new set of clothes given to survivors. Then again, they might have been Jennie's (born 1900) or Raymond Caldwell's (born 1914). Here's hoping that someday, we'll find the answer.

# ILLUSTRATION CREDITS

Page 5, Author's collection, hereafter Author. Page 6, Charles "Chuck" Caldwell, hereafter Caldwell. Page 10, Unknown artist in W. H. Sheridan McGlumphy, *Directory: Tax-Payers, Caldwell County, Missouri* (Kingston, Mo.: March, 1906), p. 85. Page 16, Author. Page 18, Fishburn Archives, Park University, hereafter Fishburn. Page 19, Fishburn. Page 20, Fishburn. Page 22, top, Fishburn; page 22, bottom, Fishburn. Page 26, Fishburn. Page 27, Fishburn. Page 35, Anne Conybeare Trach and Marcia A. Trach, hereafter Trach. Page 37, Trach. Page 39, Suda Carey. Page 43, Trach. Page 45, Caldwell. Page 54, John Robertson. Pages 62–63, Jan Hedgepeth Wright and Eleanor Wright, artists. Page 66, Author. Page 82, Author. Page 115, Front of postcard, illustration by unknown artist, courtesy of Trach; page 115, back of postcard, Trach. Page 121, Author. Page 122, Mrs. A. F. Caldwell, *Women of the Titanic Disaster* (St. Joseph, Mo.: A. W. Themanson Publishing, 1912), p. 10. Page 125, Unknown artist in *Women of the Titanic Disaster,* p. 13. Page 127, Caldwell. Page 129, Caldwell. Page 130, Author. Page 135, Author. Page 137, Kay Congleton Hedgepeth, hereafter Hedgepeth. Page 140, Bloomington Community Players Theatre scrapbook, courtesy of Bruce Parrish. Page 142, Dan Barringer and Caldwell. Page 145, Fishburn. Page 146, Caldwell. Page 148, Author. Page 150, Jennie Whit Congleton Caldwell, artist, courtesy of Hedgepeth. Page 151, Author. Page 152, Author. Page 154, Author. Page 158, Author. Page 161, Alden G. Caldwell, artist; courtesy of Hedgepeth. Page 162, Caldwell. Page 171, photo by Author.

# INDEX